PENGUIN BOOKS

A SHORT HISTORY
OF NEW ZEALAND

Gordon McLauchlan has been assiduously reading New
Zealand history, biography and fiction for more than fifty
years and for most of that time he's been writing
professional commentaries on the nation and its affairs
in magazine articles, newspaper columns and books. He
knows New Zealand as intimately and affectionately as
anyone alive and has set out in this book to provide for
the general reader a historical narrative that is personal
and colourful, and stamped with the authority of a
lifetime of deep interest.

To James and Michael McLauchlan, and Emily and Miles Gill,
in the hope they will help New Zealanders remain
the tolerant and genial people we have become.

Acknowledgement
Most of the pictures in this book come from the files of my alma mater,
the *New Zealand Herald*. I would like to thank the *Herald*'s editor-in-chief,
Gavin Ellis, and the editorial resources manager, Lauri Tapsell, for their
generous and efficient support for me and this project.

A Short History
of New Zealand

Gordon McLauchlan

PENGUIN BOOKS

PENGUIN BOOKS
Published by the Penguin Group
Penguin Books (NZ) Ltd, cnr Airborne and Rosedale Roads, Albany,
Auckland 1310, New Zealand
Penguin Books Ltd, 80 Strand, London, WC2R 0RL, England
Penguin Group (USA) Inc., 375 Hudson Street, New York, NY 10014,
United States
Penguin Books Australia Ltd, 250 Camberwell Road, Camberwell,
Victoria 3124, Australia
Penguin Books Canada Ltd, 10 Alcorn Avenue, Toronto,
Ontario, Canada M4V 3B2
Penguin Books (South Africa) (Pty) Ltd, 24 Sturdee Avenue, Rosebank,
Johannesburg 2196, South Africa
Penguin Books India (P) Ltd, 11, Community Centre, Panchsheel Park,
New Delhi 110 017, India
Penguin Books Ltd, Registered Offices: 80 Strand, London, WC2R 0RL,
England

First published by Penguin Books (NZ) Ltd, 2004
1 3 5 7 9 10 8 6 4 2

Designed by Mary Egan
Typeset@Egan-Reid.com
Printed in Australia by McPherson's Printing Group

ISBN 0 14 301908 2
A catalogue record for this book is available
from the National Library of New Zealand.

www.penguin.co.nz

CONTENTS

INTRODUCTION

HISTORIANS, BIOGRAPHERS and social commentators have picked over life in New Zealand in great detail because we are a young country, have a small and literate population and hold detailed archival material preserved since the rediscovery of the country by James Cook.

And yet, when modern events sharpen the focus on the past, scholars still find close inspection of primary sources brings new understandings. This is demonstrated by the emergence of the Treaty of Waitangi as an instrument of government policy in a bid to right what Maori have long perceived to be wrongs; and by James Belich's recent revisionist view of the New Zealand Wars that ended more than thirty years after the Treaty was signed. Research continues to throw light on the amazing story of the Polynesian exploration and settlement of the islands of the Pacific, and their eventual discovery of New Zealand.

As an avid collector and reader of old and new histories and social commentaries, and as a professional writer for fifty years, I embarked on this project to introduce our country's story to general readers and to students. I've tried to tell what previous writers – fuelled by the prejudices and conventional wisdom of their day – have said about our past, and, in some cases, what they haven't said; although all of us, writers and professional historians, are trapped to some extent in our own time and place.

This is a short and personal narrative, but I believe it is as up-to-date and accurate as one can be in such a confined space. My sincerest hope is that I stimulate an interest readers will then pursue in longer and more detailed books on the people and events that have made New Zealanders of all ethnic origins the tolerant, liberated, hard-working people I believe we are.

Gordon McLauchlan

Chapter One:

THE YOUNG COUNTRY

THE EARTH IS about 4600 million years old, and the land that is now New Zealand was until only 140 million years ago a tiny piece of Gondwanaland, one of two supercontinents. The other was Laurasia. Over the aeons, Gondwanaland broke up into Antarctica, New Zealand, Australia, New Guinea, New Caledonia, Africa, Arabia, South America, Madagascar and India.

About eighty million years ago, the land mass that was later to become Australia and New Zealand moved northwards from the Antarctic into approximately the region of the globe the two countries occupy now. New Zealand's more

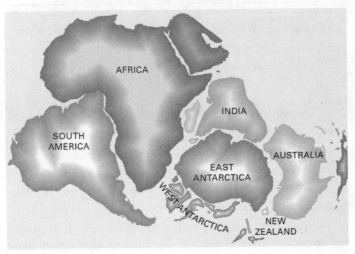

Gondwanaland was, according to the theory of continental drift, the southern super-continent from which New Zealand, Australia, Antarctica, South America, India and Africa split and, over geological aeons, took up their present positions on the globe. It was originally named Gondwana by Austrian geologist Eduard Suess who first hypothesised continental drift on the basis of the similarity of flora and fauna among the southern land masses.
(Terralink International)

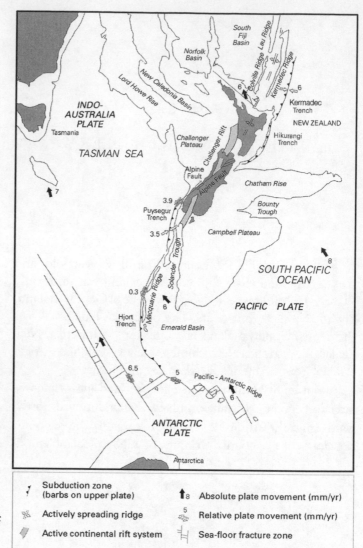

The earth's surface is broken into seven large and many small plates which move only a few inches a year. The boundary of the Indo-Australia and Pacific plates – where they collide – moves across the South Island from the west and along the east coast of the North Island creating the friction that leads to earthquakes and volcanic activity.
(Terralink International)

particular history began twelve million years ago as a long, narrow strip of land sitting in its present position. Since then, earth movements, volcanic activity, dramatic climate changes, erosion and receding and advancing sea levels have all contributed to the shape it became about ten thousand years ago and is today.

But the earth's crust is still on the move. The manifestations of the shifting of the surface are earthquakes, volcanoes and smaller geothermal vents. All three occur in New Zealand because it's at the interface of two gigantic pieces of moving crust – the Pacific and the Indo-Australia plates. And so our history has been tumultuous, full of geological sound and fury signifying a country on the tectonic edge.

Since Europeans began to settle here two hundred years ago, five cataclysms have sounded a warning that this green and pleasant land sits on volatile foundations. The first was an 1848 earthquake in Wellington which frightened some people into leaving the young town and persuaded those who stayed to build in timber. In 1855, another, more powerful earthquake in the Wellington region lifted the coastline two metres from the sea. Experts calculate it was the only New Zealand quake in modern times to reach magnitude eight on the Richter scale. As you fly above the capital, you may see the fault line running straight as a die north along the Hutt Road and on along the eastern edge of the Hutt Valley's western hills.

By 1886 the Pink and White Terraces had become so famous that many notable visitors to New Zealand ventured to the shore of Lake Rotomahana in the central North Island to see them. That year they were destroyed when Mount Tarawera blew apart in a huge eruption, killing an estimated 153 people.

In 1886, Mount Tarawera, in the central North Island, erupted from three craters, killing an estimated 153 people, leaving huge craggy scars, and burying the Pink and White Terraces. The terraces, even by then, were a world-renowned tourist attraction that had drawn the admiration of English novelist Anthony Trollope and the Duke of Edinburgh, Prince Albert (in 1870), among others. They

were formed by the natural crystallisation of silica deposited as water from a boiling lake situated above cooled down. They now lie deep in a grave of cold, hard lava.

In 1929, an earthquake at Murchison in the north of the South Island killed seventeen people, virtually obliterated the small settlement, and lifted one part of a road four metres above the other. Only two years later, an earthquake in Hawke's Bay killed 256 people – 161 in Napier, ninety-three

11

in Hastings and two in Wairoa – and raised sixteen square kilometres of land from the sea.

About a hundred earthquakes shift us around each year but only one or two are large enough to be felt.

New Zealand is an especially young country on two counts:

▶ Geologically, most rocks are less than a hundred million years old and even the oldest are younger than a thousand million years, representing a short period in geological time.

▶ The length of human occupancy is certainly less than 1500 years (possibly only 800), compared, for example, with 40,000 years in Australia. New Zealand was the last large land mass in the world to be settled.

Geographical isolation over a long period made this country a kind of nature reserve for animal and plant groups that did not survive the evolutionary wars among the species in larger, more accessible places.

Thus the tuatara has outlived the other members of its *Rhyncocephalia* family in other countries by a hundred million years. Because predatory mammals were unknown, some birds (the huia and kakapo, for example) climbed sedately among the trees, while others flew in short bursts (piopio, the New Zealand thrush) and a few just stayed down there on the ground (kiwi and moa).

Sea birds, in numbers hard to imagine today, wheeled in

The Napier earthquake on 3 February 1931, remains New Zealand's worst natural disaster with a death toll of 256 throughout Hawke's Bay, 161 of them in the city. The devastation seen here soon afterwards meant Napier was rebuilt in the prevailing Art Deco style but it wasn't until fifty years later that these buildings began to be exploited as the tourist attraction it has become.

huge flocks around coastal waters, many of them fishing far out to sea. Others migrated along age-old transcontinental routes, resurfacing some islands with their guano when they rested. All these birds in their huge numbers were key guides to Polynesian navigators.

When Polynesian explorers arrived they found fish and game aplenty, including an abundance of sea mammals around the coast. The birds, mostly untroubled by enemies for centuries, were easy targets to support the hunting and gathering culture that quickly developed. Maori had easy access to protein but fruit and carbohydrates were scarce compared with what was available on the tropical islands they had come from.

By the time European explorers arrived, many bird species were extinct. Others have disappeared since and some are under threat today.

Chapter Two:

THE ORIGINS OF THE MAORI

Egypt is at the height of its cultural brilliance and imperial power under the eighteenth dynasty of Pharaohs.

The Babylonian Empire is in decline.

The Greeks are moving from the Caspian Sea into the eastern Mediterranean, the new home in which they will flourish as one of history's most enlightened civilisations.

The Phoenicians have reached Malta to become the predominant traders in the Mediterranean.

Stonehenge is still the centre of religious worship for people in southern England.

THAT WAS MORE than 3000 years ago. In what we now call the Middle East, long-settled agricultural people had built up trade to a level that demanded simple accounting which in turn led to a primitive form of writing; so, from then on, we know something of their lives and the way they thought.

At that same time, on the other side of the Earth, a group of vigorous sailors known in history as the Lapita People, best identified by archaeologists from their ornamented pottery, are settling on Vanua Levu, in the Fiji group, an island speck in the immensity of the Pacific Ocean. They have already completed sea journeys beyond the imagination of the Egyptians, the Greeks or the sailing-trading Phoenicians.

The Lapita People's life was never settled or sedentary, so they have no writing. Modern scholars of language, archaeology, anthropology, biology, botany and physics have constructed what we know of them.

Over a period of 50,000 years, since the earliest human voyaging, the ancestors of these people had gradually developed what became matchless maritime skills in the safe waters that washed around the long peninsulas and dense archipelagoes of South-East Asia. Then, quite suddenly, carrying way-back genes from Asia and Africa, they sprang out into the Pacific across the top of Papua New Guinea, and swooped along the Bismarck Archipelago.

These migrant groups travelled in outrigger canoes built to carry themselves, their livestock and their chattels at speeds of around four knots, probing 5000 kilometres to the east, island by island, through seas pacific only in name.

By 1200 BC, they had colonised the Fijian and Tongan groups, the Samoas, Uvea, Futuna, the western fringe of the northern Cook Islands, Niue, the Tokelaus and other, smaller islands, all previously uninhabited. They had become an isolated, mid-Pacific maritime community. During that last

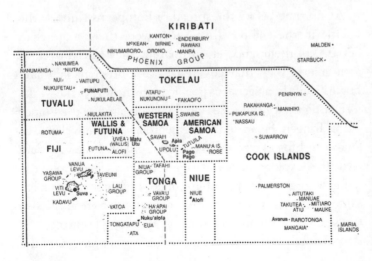

The Polynesians had colonised the previously uninhabited Fijian and Tongan groups, the Samoas, Uvea, Futuna, the western Cook Islands and other small islands by about 1200 BC.
(Map courtesy Hawaii Geographic Society, Honolulu 96806-1698)

15

surge from the eastern periphery of Asia into the Pacific, their numbers were so small and they moved so swiftly over such great distances that they emerged beyond the reach of pandemic diseases such as malaria.

The Polynesians' cultural origins are obscure but they were descended from the 'Lapita People' who moved into the Pacific from the west and north-west and were distinguished by pottery with distinctive motifs, and by tattooing chisels and fishhooks. The pottery was widespread in the western Pacific region but the Polynesians abandoned pottery making, probably because suitable materials became unavailable in their new island homes.
(Te Papa Tongarewa, Museum of NZ)

Their cultural origins are obscure except they were heirs to a Lapita tradition, which means they were identifiable from their pottery, tattooing chisels, and distinctive adzes and fishhooks. They also traded in obsidian. Although much of their pottery was plain and utilitarian, some carried characteristic decorations, executed with great artistry – carved and stamped with simple parallel lines, teeth-like shapes, curves and concentrically arranged motifs, some representing the human form. This pottery was also widespread in Melanesia, including Papua New Guinea, the Solomon Islands and New Caledonia, and the style echoes back through South-East Asia, particularly to Taiwan and the Philippines, probably homelands of their remote ancestors.

In their mid-Pacific isolation over several hundred years, they adapted to their changed environment, discarded pottery-making and evolved into a distinctive people with their own language and way of living. They became the Polynesians.

At no time before the spread of Europeans through the Pacific in the eighteenth century were there more than 800,000 of them; and yet, ultimately, they spread over an area greater than that covered by any other racially and linguistically homogeneous people in the history of the world.

During their regular, seasonal voyages among the islands of the Tongan, Fijian and Samoan groups, they developed to an astonishing degree two skills that enabled them to dare to further explore the world's largest ocean. These were the manufacture of sturdy double-hulled, highly manoeuvrable sailing canoes, and navigational techniques to read the sky, the sea, the wind and sea bird migrations – knowing how they changed and recurred during the various seasons of the

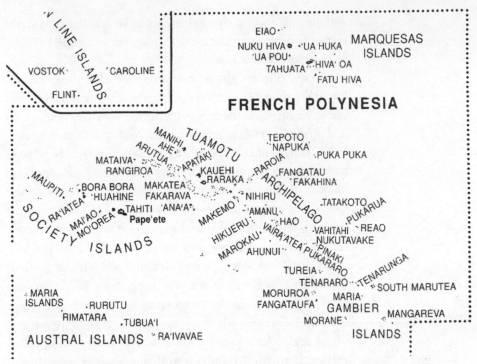

LINE ISLANDS

VOSTOK· ·CAROLINE

FLINT·

EIAO· ·
NUKU HIVA ● ·UA HUKA
·UA POU·
TAHUATA ·HIVA· OA
·FATU HIVA

MARQUESAS
ISLANDS

FRENCH POLYNESIA

MANIHI· TUAMOTU
AHE· TEPOTO
ARUTUA ·NAPUKA
APATAKI ·PUKA PUKA
MATAIVA· RAROIA
RANGIROA KAUEHI FANGATAU
BORA BORA MAKATEA RARAKA ARCHIPELAGO FAKAHINA
MAUPITI· HUAHINE FAKARAVA NIHIRU
RA'IATEA· MAKEMO· AMANU· ·TATAKOTO ·PUKARUA
MAI'AO· TAHITI 'ANA'A· HAO ·VAHITAHI ·REAO
MO'OREA Pape'ete HIKUERU· VAIRA'ATEA NUKUTAVAKE
SOCIETY MAROKAU· PUKARARO ·PINAKI
AHUNUI·
ISLANDS TUREIA·
TENARARO· ·TENARUNGA ·SOUTH MARUTEA
MARIA MORUROA· MARIA·
ISLANDS ·RURUTU FANGATAUFA· GAMBIER ·MANGAREVA
·RIMATARA MORANE·
·TUBUA'I ISLANDS
AUSTRAL ISLANDS ·RA'IVAVAE

year. And because the sea birds had the islands to themselves, virtually free of predators, they proliferated to a population probably unmatched anywhere else in the world, limited only by their food supply.

The Polynesian navigators became so familiar with their natural environment they could journey around their islands with confidence. Thus the apt name the region was given was from the Greek: *poly* meaning many, and *nesoi* islands. By the time they found a new island, they had memorised the winds, currents and astral charts that had taken them there to prepare for two-way travel, bedding the instructions into folklore for the benefit of succeeding expeditions.

Before the birth of Christ, small groups had stepping-stoned their way across the atolls and small rocky islands of the eastern Pacific to the Marquesas, the Society Group and the long string of the Tuamotu Archipelago. The further eastward they moved, the more they needed to refine their navigational skills and canoe technology because the islands were now more scattered and smaller – in many cases, atolls,

The next wave of settlement took the Polynesian navigators eastwards to the Marquesas, the Society group and the Tuamotu Archipelago about 2000 years ago. A consensus among modern scholars is that the main thrust of the migration moved from the western Pacific to the Fiji-Samoa-Tonga region, then eastwards to Tahiti, the Marquesas and the Tuamotu Archipelago before sailing across the wind to Hawaii, Easter Island and New Zealand. (Map courtesy Hawaii Geographic Society, Honolulu 96806-1968) with just whispers of cloud above them, or creating only slight shifts of current to indicate their presence, crouched as they were so low on the horizon.

These explorers almost certainly probed further east and found South and Central America, already inhabited on land uncongenial to islanders. Some returned with the sweet potato and other plants. Some may have stayed and been absorbed. When they could find no more islands to the east, they began to sail across the wind and thus discovered and populated Hawaii to the north and Rapa Nui (Easter Island) to the south. Then they explored the south-west and found New Zealand. They also landed on the coast of Australia but encountered an alien landscape and long-established inhabitants.

So the Polynesians became distinctively who they are in the central Pacific after arriving there about 3000 years ago from the west. Wide disagreement reigns over the timing of their movements – whether they stayed in the Fiji, Samoa, Tonga region for a long period or whether they soon pushed eastwards to the Marquesas and the Society Islands; and when, after that, they discovered the Hawaiian Group, Easter Island and New Zealand. But there is general agreement on the probability of that sequence of settlement.

That is an outline of the Polynesian story as it is understood today. But we have arrived at it after a long journey through myth and misapprehension. What we are today colours to some degree how we see what we used to be. This story is conditioned by here and now, but we have the advantage of incremental gains of fairly reliable information from a range of scholars as the years go by; so if I'm dismissive of what now seems like goofy speculation in the past, it may be that new scientific information accrued in the future will make our contemporary reconstructions look more primitive and subjective than we think.

After Stephenson Percy Smith died at his home in New Plymouth in April 1922, the *Taranaki Daily News* published an obituary which said that when the biographies of the truly great men of New Zealand came to be written, his name would be close to the summit of the scroll of fame. That may seem hyperbolic now but for a long time Smith was the most famous and respected of the many New Zealanders investigating what was then a pervasive and enduring mystery: the origins of the Maori.

James Cook and those aboard the *Endeavour* in the second half of the eighteenth century were among the first outsiders to comprehend the extent of the long-distance voyaging of the Polynesians. A Tahitian priest aboard the *Endeavour*, Tupaia, made it obvious that not only did the Pacific Islanders look similar but they spoke closely related languages. He also knew the general location of many of the inhabited islands. Cook, the greatest navigator of his time, belonged to the first generation able to calculate longitude precisely with the use of accurate shipboard instruments and navigational tables and, after his first voyage, chronometers. He could thus pinpoint his position anywhere on the globe. He and his companions realised that when Polynesians were voyaging around the Pacific in large but relatively fragile double canoes, the most expert sailors in countries that had the technology to build large ships were still nervous about losing sight of land.

Although regional sailing was still common among Polynesians in the eighteenth century, long-haul voyaging had stopped. Cook and others began wrestling with the question of whether the islands had been settled by calculated expeditions of exploration, or by unplanned voyages – canoes attempting regional journeys, getting lost and blundering into previously undiscovered islands; or by suicidally dangerous journeys, sailing blindly into the ocean because of exile for political or religious reasons.

The movement of peoples around the great land masses in other parts of the globe had ready explanations. Forced by population pressures, wars or by the restless spirit of adventure that is so characteristically human, migrations across Africa, Asia and Europe could be made on foot. Asians had moved into the Americas across Bering Strait when there was a land bridge. Australia's Aborigines had arrived as early as 40,000 years ago, either on foot when the island continent was not quite an island, or in small canoes across the relatively short distances to visible coastlines; or both. The Vikings made daring and controlled voyages from Scandinavia to the British Isles during the first millennium, and then to Iceland, Greenland and perhaps North America. But these journeys were to extended coastlines.

Compared with discovering Hawaii from Tahiti or the Marquesas and probably sailing back, finding the coastline of America would have been a doddle for any vessel well built and well provisioned enough to keep sailing westward across the North Atlantic. Columbus bravely pushed out into the Atlantic more than a thousand years after the Polynesians had reached all the way across the Pacific.

The origins of Polynesians and the nature of their diaspora seemed stranger than fiction a century ago but, as usual with human beings, the want of details led mystified romantics to scramble around and make some up. They conjectured wildly with varying degrees of plausibility. Navigators, geologists, linguists, botanists, archaeologists and anthropologists weighed in with theories, as did ethnologists who deconstructed religions, cultural practices, and the song and story of these widely dispersed groups. They slugged it out for years.

The theories ranged from the fairly plausible to the absurd. The Polynesians were one of the tribes of Israel. They came here from Ancient Egypt, from Arabia, from Madagascar, from southern China, from India, from North, Central and South America, arrived in eastern Polynesia as a group of migrating Caucasians via what is now British Columbia.

Early missionary leader Samuel Marsden, and Oxford graduate and eminent academic at the University of Canterbury John Macmillan Brown are just two examples of intelligent, educated men who groped around and came up with explanations of gross improbability. Marsden decided New Zealand Maori had 'sprung from some dispersed Jews at some period or other' because of similarity between selected religious customs, and what he considered cultural similarities, such as: 'They have like the Jews a great natural turn for traffic; they will buy and sell anything they have got.' It was Brown who declared, 'Caucasians had reached the Pacific coast of Asia and British Columbia long before the Mongoloids' and the only non-Caucasian influence on the Polynesians was 'Negroid, brought in by the last immigrants and conquerors'.

Yet another theory that had its brief day until emphatically denounced by geologists was that Polynesians had spread around a huge Pacific land mass, or along chains of large islands, which had then sunk beneath the ocean, except for mountain tops. Belief in the idea of a huge southern continent had long been held by many northern hemisphere geographers who considered it would be needed in the southern hemisphere to balance the weight of Asia and Europe in the north. Abel Janszoon Tasman's main task during his 1642 voyage was to find 'Staten Landt'. He and his navigator, Frans Jacobszoon Visscher, thought they had done that when they found the west coast of New Zealand. More than a century later, the indefatigable Cook sailed south and west of New Zealand to the edge of Antarctica in search of such a continent.

Stephenson Percy Smith, amateur ethnologist and author of Hawaiki: The Original Home of the Maori, *spent much of his life researching Maori traditions and whakapapa, speculating on the migration of Polynesians and on the nature and timing of their expeditions to settle New Zealand.*

While anthropologists and other intellectuals, professional and amateur, turned aside from their day jobs to conjecture glibly on the mystery, Percy Smith spent a lifetime assiduously studying the genealogies, folklore and traditions of Polynesians. As a young surveyor, he travelled throughout

New Zealand, learning Maori and listening to the song and story of iwi. He traced the origin of the Polynesians back to Caucasians who migrated down through India. He constructed a detailed history of their voyaging around the Pacific, complete with names and dates, almost all of it based on the traditions of New Zealand Maori and Cook Islanders, with some input from other East Polynesian groups. His work may be outmoded and most of it discredited now but it was once powerfully influential. The four editions of his major work, *Hawaiki: The Original Home of the Maori*, dominated popular thinking and New Zealand school curricula for at least the first half of the twentieth century. That is why the *Taranaki Daily News* presumed history would enshrine him as a truly great New Zealander.

Smith was born in England and moved to New Plymouth with his family when he was nine. In 1889, he became the Colony's Surveyor General and Secretary for Lands and Mines. In 1892, he helped found the Polynesian Society, and was co-editor or editor of the society's journal until his death. He was essentially a Victorian who wore fustian three-piece suits, complete with a watch-chain across his belly and a white handkerchief tucked into his top pocket. During Smith's mature years, it was difficult to view Maori with any kind of objective historical eye. Towards the end of the nineteenth century, some anthropologists were talking of them in the past tense, convinced they would take the same road to extinction as the Moriori. Thus, as Pakeha reflected with affection and guilt on their virtues, Maori took on the aura of the Noble Savage.

Smith used Maori and Polynesian traditions for *what* happened and whakapapa for *when*, estimating historical time by counting back the generations. He actually got quite a lot right but took insufficient account of mythology's imaginative poetry and of the corruption of traditions that occurred almost immediately Maori came into contact with Europeans. Missionaries had brought the new mythology of the *Bible*, some of which was imported into the traditions; and Maori, being a curious and adventurous people, were quickly travelling around the Pacific on European ships, talking with European sailors and Polynesians of other communities. In an oral culture stories are living organisms. Clear judgement of what was original pre-European material and what was new or adapted quickly became impossible. Also, genealogies are manipulated in the interests of political relationships and power. Some claim Smith was too subjective in his approach to traditions and easily confused because he wasn't a professional scholar. He may have been both subjective and confused – but then so were some of the scholars, especially those working outside their professional disciplines.

In *Hawaiki*, Smith claimed Polynesians were able to navigate the Pacific Ocean in all directions with relative ease. About 925, he wrote, an explorer from Raiatea in the Society Group named Kupe, during a visit to Rarotonga, discovered what he named Aotearoa after noticing land birds flying in from the south-west to winter in the central Pacific. He found New Zealand, circumnavigated both islands and took the news back to Tahiti. It was, however, more than 200 years before the next canoe arrived with settlers. The immigrants were led by Toi-te-huatahi. They found a group of people here who had Melanesian blood but spoke Polynesian. These were the Moriori who were driven to the Chathams by the more vigorous Toi and his companions. In 1350, the Great Fleet arrived from Rarotonga, a flotilla of the canoes to which Maori traditionally traced back their Aotearoa arrival. The Great Fleet theory was lodged into history for more than half a century. Some school textbooks carried on their covers a reproduction of the painting by Charles F. Goldie and L. J. Steele called *The Arrival of the Maoris in New Zealand*, depicting an emaciated, bulge-eyed complement of Polynesians packed into a double canoe with one man near the prow pointing to land ahead. This melodramatic symbol of the Great Fleet, painted in 1898, accurately represented the beliefs of the time, awash as they were with sentimentality.

As the twentieth century progressed, linguists, ethnologists, archaeologists and anthropologists continued the steady accumulation of information that began to give scholarly substance to the Polynesian story. Among them were another New Plymouth surveyor, H. D. Skinner, younger than Smith but a foundation member of the Polynesian Society, and his son W. H., who graduated as a lawyer but professionally followed his interest as an ethnologist; Roger Duff, an archaeologist who discovered the moa-hunter site on Wairau Bar; and Maori anthropologist Sir Peter Buck, who became director of the Bishop Museum in Hawaii in 1936. Before his career as an ethnologist, Buck had been a politician and a medical doctor who worked in the area of public health. But the gradual progress of these professionals was over-shadowed after World War II by two revisionists whose theories were given wide publicity.

The first was a Norwegian anthropologist, Thor Heyerdahl, who built a balsa raft he named *Kon-Tiki*, and sailed it from Callao in Peru to Puka-Puka in the Tuamotu Archipelago. Heyerdahl had spent time in the Marquesas where he had learnt of a tradition that led him to believe the Polynesians came from South America. He backed it up with claims about the origins of Polynesian art and of plants; and he had as an ally the sweet potato, forefather of New Zealand's kumara, which came from Central or South America. What served Heyerdahl well was that his account of the journey, *The Kon-Tiki Expedition*, first published in 1948, was a gripping read and became a best-seller. But after its period of worldwide popularity his theory gradually evaporated in the heat of superior scholarship.

Then, in 1956, *Ancient Voyagers in the Pacific* by New Zealander Andrew Sharp was published. The author insisted the Pacific was settled by what he called 'accidental' voyages (a term he later modified to 'one-way' voyages), and that none of the early mariners could navigate accurately enough to sail over long distances with any hope of return. Sharp, who refined his theory in *Ancient Voyagers in Polynesia* (1963), accepted that surprisingly ambitious regional voyages were

Immediately after World War II, Norwegian anthropologist Thor Heyerdahl attempted to prove that the Polynesians came from South America by sailing a balsa raft from Peru to Puka-Puka in the Tuamotus. His account of the expedition, a book called Kon-Tiki, *became a best-seller and lent wide popular support to his claim, but his theories have not survived scholarly examination.*

common because he knew that when Cook reached the Pacific, Tahitians were still sailing within the Society Group and the Tuamotus, and Tongans, Fijians and Samoans were also visiting and trading among themselves. He discounted, however, that there had ever been two-way, long-haul expeditions to seek, find and settle in such destinations as Hawaii, Easter Island and New Zealand. He questioned claims by early European explorers that various Polynesian communities knew of the existence and direction of faraway islands.

Sharp's books had none of the affable, high readability of Heyerdahl's. They had the thunder of polemics about them; but they did raise a stir and encourage affronted contemporary Polynesian and Pakeha scholars to confirm with more evidence claims that long-distance exploration had been possible.

No one can explain with any confidence why planned, distant voyaging had ended by the eighteenth century, but modern navigators, replicating as far as is possible the traditional sailing instructions, have shown that long two-way journeys of exploration were possible. During the 1960s, an intrepid New Zealand physician, David Lewis, in his catamaran, and in the 1970s and 1980s, Hawaii's Nainoa Thompson and others in a double canoe, sailed confidently around the Pacific. Of course, they did have access to reservoirs of modern knowledge including meteorological and oceanic records that Polynesian navigators would have had to carry in their heads and transfer from one generation to another.

One long-lasting conundrum was how could exploration have gone from west to east when steady and, for long periods of the year, unremitting trade winds blow from the east and thus into the teeth of voyagers from the central Pacific to the Marquesas and Tahiti? Well, modern researchers say that was an advantage because expeditions could set out eastwards during the relatively brief periods when wind came from the

Another anthropologist who promoted a revisionist theory of Polynesian settlement was New Zealander Andrew Sharp who claimed in Ancient Voyagers in the Pacific (1956) that long-haul voyages were 'accidental' because Polynesian sailors could not possibly have navigated accurately enough to have any hope of returning. His Ancient Voyagers in Polynesia (1963) modified his views somewhat but he still claimed long-haul, two-way expeditions to seek, find and settle distant destinations such as Easter Island, Hawaii and New Zealand were impossible.

David Lewis, an intrepid New Zealand physician, was one of a group of sailors who, during the 1960s, successfully followed the supposed routes of Polynesian long-haul expeditions, replicating as far as possible traditional sailing instructions without using modern technology. They claimed to have proved such planned journeys of discovery and settlement would have been possible.

west, and even across the wind, confident they could sail back home if they found no new land when the reliable easterlies returned.

Always working against the unplanned drift theory was the need for canoes to have carried reasonably substantial settlement populations on their expeditions, complete with plants and livestock. Also, a computerised investigation strongly suggested drift voyages from eastern Polynesia to new islands could not have occurred under anything like normal conditions.

Contemporary opinion among scholars still diverges on the matter of the timing of the migratory voyages, on the order in which the various island groups were settled, and on how many migrating parties there were from which departure points. Was Hawaii settled first from the Marquesas or Tahiti? Archaeology suggests settlers ultimately came from both sources. Did the progenitors of Maori come directly from the Marquesas or Tahiti as the linguistics evidence suggests, or via the southern Cook Islands – Rarotonga or Mangaia? When did they come and how many canoes arrived over the years?

But despite these questions, the amount of agreement is striking. Linguistics and archaeology have established a broad pattern – Polynesians did not sail into the central Pacific as a formed cultural group, they evolved there from the Lapita People. They did develop the canoe technology and the navigational skills to make long expeditions that searched for new homelands and in many cases returned. And those expeditions did move from central Polynesia to eastern Polynesia and from there to Easter Island, Hawaii and New Zealand.

Why would expeditions embark on such enterprises? Perhaps because that is what they had always done. They may have been encouraged by population pressures exacerbated by drought or cyclonic devastation. Groups may have been expelled or have decided to emigrate because of political ambitions or religious conflicts at home – much as European groups faced the dangers and deprivation of emigration to

America in the sixteenth and seventeenth centuries.

Polynesian expeditions would have had major economic ramifications on their communities. The construction of an ocean-going canoe and the provisioning for a long voyage required massive capital input. No one would deny some expeditions were lost forever because unseasonable weather so seriously disrupted sailing traditions that re-establishing their position would have been impossible without modern navigational equipment. But the fact is they sailed where no one had sailed before, and who would believe island communities would allocate scarce resources for regular, lotto-like, suicide-style missions into the unknown, enough of them to populate by accident the huge area of Polynesian settlement.

About 1000 years ago – perhaps, according to the latest scholarship, only 800 – the *Vikings of the Pacific* as Peter Buck called the Polynesians, set out for New Zealand. It was almost certainly their last major discovery and in many ways their most difficult. What did they find?

Chapter Three:

DISCOVERY

O UR EARLY HISTORY requires an act of the imagination by writers and readers creating pictures around the precious little we know; so, think of a double-hulled canoe with about twenty people aboard approaching this alien coast a month after departure from a small tropical island. The women are still tending animals and plants. The canoe has slid down below the Tropic of Capricorn most probably from the southern Cook Islands, but possibly from the Society Group, or the Tuamotus, or even the Marquesas. The navigator is weary after searching the skies every waking moment, reading new winds and ocean swells less predictable than he is used to.

Every year a steady nor'easterly arrives in the region in early summer, before the hurricane season, and the lore says it usually stays long enough to promise an exploration for new islands. The sailing plan the navigator devised, probing for the south-west corner of the ocean, seems to have paid off, but if these migrants find nothing they will try to sail across the wind, northwards, to where they know the skies. A gamble – but not without calculation.

But most of their anxieties disappeared days ago with so many signals in the sea and the air telling them they were approaching land, and a sizeable island at that. Here it is – with no familiar reef or lagoon, only cold, rock-strewn sea reaching up to a beach backed by brooding, deep-green trees, steep cliffs glowering over either end. Colours change as the sunshine comes and goes through broken, fast-moving clouds. The solid forest runs along the visible coast each way and climbs over the crest of the encroaching hills as far as anyone can see. High excitement charges them as they reach a new home – but it looks very different. That brings an under-current of fear. Who or what may lurk inside the green wall or behind the hills? They see ragged clouds of small birds suddenly swirling in the air out of the trees and settling again a few metres away. Perhaps, if it is late in the day, they will stay anchored offshore in case the darkness brings unwelcome visitors; or are they so tired, so cramped, so thirsty they will take their chance on the beach?

Thus Polynesians discovered New Zealand. No one is sure precisely when it was; or how often the dangerous expedition into the swirling temperate zone to the south-west was undertaken; or whether those who reached New Zealand ever made it back. One thing seems certain, though: a fleet of canoes could not have kept together on such a journey in the formation of a Great Fleet.

Polynesian voyaging seems to have been at a peak in the early years of the second millennium, with many exploring expeditions, followed by settlement, where habitable islands were found. Scientific evidence suggests the regional climate may have been a degree or two warmer in the thirteenth century, and the ocean in the southern temperate zone perhaps less dangerous as a result. As recently as the early 1990s, educated guesses on the date of settlement went back as far as the ninth century and beyond, but archaeologists have lately been mainly responsible for bringing the date forward. They have found no evidence of a human presence here before AD 1250, and expert consensus puts arrival at around that time. One clue is a fishing lure found at Tairua, on the east coast of the Coromandel Peninsula, and now in the Auckland War Memorial Museum. It is made from the tropical black-lipped pearl shell that doesn't exist in New Zealand waters, so must have been brought here from outside. Radiocarbon dating puts its manufacture at late thirteenth to mid-fourteenth century.

As the date of Polynesian settlement comes forward, the likelihood grows of a number of settlement voyages rather than just one or two because estimates of the Maori population when Cook arrived in the eighteenth century are somewhere between a hundred and a hundred and fifty thousand.

At the peak of long-distance voyaging, Polynesian navigators probably located new islands and returned with sailing instructions, enabling settlement canoes to make at least several journeys. Traces of temporary Polynesian settlement have been found on Raoul Island in the Kermadecs, possibly a staging post on the way to New Zealand. But, at best, these are educated guesses made in the absence, yet anyway, of more complete skeletons of information on which to hang the flesh of theories.

If Maori arrived in the thirteenth century, wars, big and small, were ravaging Europe and Asia. King John makes war on the Welsh, and Genghis Khan sacks Beijing.

There the newcomers were – in an outpost of eastern Polynesian culture but in a land so big, so different. The weather was more variable, with longer days during the summer, shorter in winter. Temperatures ranged from tolerably cool in the north to dangerously cold in the far south.

The Polynesians faced a drastic adaptation because of these differences in climate, environment and economy. They brought with them tenderly cared for kumara (long, thin, white tubers compared with today's varieties), yam, taro, the paper mulberry, a cabbage tree, the gourd and almost certainly tropical plants such as the coconut, breadfruit and banana that didn't survive the move. At least one expedition must have ridden the nor'easter in late spring, landed on the east coast north of Hawke's Bay and made clearings in sandy, well-drained soil to get their kumara planted as early summer warmed the ground. For their treasured kumara, yam and taro plants, which grow all year round in the tropics, survival would have been a near thing as the immigrants adjusted to seasonal planting and growing.

The settlers also brought in their boats the kiore (rat), possibly as stowaways, and the kuri (dog), but what happened to fowls and pigs, staple domestic animals in tropical Polynesia? These four animals are found throughout Polynesia, except for New Zealand, and Easter Island (where the remains of only chicken and kiore are found). Not hard to imagine that the few fowls were eaten immediately or failed to adapt quickly enough, and were left uncared for once the local species of land birds were seen and tasted. But no one can account for the absence of pigs, so much a Polynesian delicacy. One possibility is pigs didn't arrive because of their lack of stamina and robustness for voyaging; another is they arrived but didn't survive because of the absence of their basic food: garden waste, from breadfruit for example. And again, the abundance of seals and large, meaty birds would have made the new settlers less concerned about their demise. Another suggestion is the journeys to New Zealand and Easter Island were so long and arduous, the pigs were eaten as food supplies aboard canoes ran low.

The Polynesian rat, or kiore, is the only animal found throughout the islands, carried on expeditions possibly as stowaways but also as a source of food. Only the kiore and chicken made it to Easter Island, and only the kiore and kuri, or dog, survived in New Zealand to European times. Elsewhere in Polynesia the pig and the chicken were domesticated animals used for food.
(Department of Conservation)

When did these settlers become Maori?

They remained distinctively Polynesian as a race but over the centuries adapted culturally to this environment – reshaping behaviour and beliefs in a larger and more diverse landscape. So urgent was the need to adapt, their new home probably impinged on the fabric of their lives, including their art and literature, within a generation or two.

Archaeologists have read much from stone, bone and shell tools, fishhooks and other artefacts found at middens both

Rock drawings found in the limestone hills near Weka Pass are dated around the fifteenth century, at a time when game birds were still plentiful enough for Maori to be hunters and gatherers.
(Te Papa Tongarewa, Museum of NZ)

A Maori preparing flax in an early post-European period. Visitors remarked on the sophistication of flax processing by women into products of special flexibility and strength.
(Te Papa Tongarewa, Museum of NZ)

ancient and recent. These finds confirm that the early settlers originated in eastern Polynesia; that trade around both main islands existed in obsidian, basalts, greenstone and other base materials; that wood-working tools developed gradually to a high level as Maori took advantage of their plentiful new resource; that the 'Moa-Hunters' – as the early hunter-gatherers were labelled by anthropologists – were profligate with their easy game. Wood, however, is perishable material once it is cut, so little can be read from what's left – except from small and beautiful works of art found preserved in swamps.

Clothing and shelter would have been imperatives for the new arrivals from the tropics. The superiority of flax would have been recognised fairly early for use in cordage and clothing. Joseph Banks and other early visitors remarked on the sophistication of flax processing by Maori women into products of special flexibility and strength.

Broadly, pre-European Maori culture was divided into two periods: the original, adaptive Archaic style of subsisting on seals, moa and similar game, and the rich coastal marine life; and the Classic style of the later period after the advanced techniques for storing kumara gave northern tribes more leisure. By the time the European rediscoverers arrived, the arts of carving and weaving and the construction of whare and coastal waka were at a high level.

The new arrivals immediately became hunters and gatherers rather than the gardeners and fishermen they had been on their tropical islands. The kumara wouldn't grow south of Banks Peninsula and needed special care in any place where winter lingered and autumn came early. The settlers would have been faced with a shortage of carbohydrate in their diet, because it was many years before the bracken rhizome began to be eaten. The evidence for this is in the extreme erosion of teeth that is not evident among the earliest bodies found.

The fat from birds and, particularly, seals would have provided energy food. The abundance of game, especially in the forests of the South Island, was a luxurious distraction.

The big birds, with no previous predators, were not shy of humans, at first at least, and were cumbersome movers. Early Maori were so overwhelmed by abundance they were prodigal hunters; so within a few hundred years, seal numbers were down and they had so seriously eaten into the game stock that twelve species of moa, a native duck, a goose, a swan, a woodhen (about the size of a kiwi) and some poor flyers among the tree birds (the huia, for example, with its much prized feathers) became endangered and then extinct.

Moa species, from the ratite family, ranged from turkey-size up to *Dinornis giganteus*, which was about two metres tall at the shoulder. The native eagle, possibly the biggest eagle that ever existed, died out as well from a shortage of food: small flightless birds and large-bird carrion. Kiore and kuri possibly played a role in the extinction of the land birds by feeding on eggs. Whatever the cause, four or five hundred years ago, Maori had to make the transition back to gardening and fishing.

Hapu, or extended families, which had lived in bush huts as they moved around in search of prey, began to settle in kainga, or villages, and lay claim to land on which they could best grow kumara – north-facing with good drainage – and clear areas by fire for the bracken to grow and make their rhizomes available. Advances were made, mainly in the north of the country, in the cultivation and particularly the storage of kumara. Maori never lost the knack of knocking up temporary huts with light frames stuck into the ground, walled and thatched with reeds, as they went on fishing expeditions; but as they settled in one place they built more substantial houses on timber frames in inverted Vs with verandahs in the front.

One seventeenth-century village near the coast in the Bay of Plenty has been meticulously worked over by archaeologists. The evidence points to a community of households, side by side around the shore of a small lake, each with a separate house, storehouse and yard area. After they settled

This impression of the kiwi and the extinct moa was drawn by Dr Ferdinand von Hochstetter, a German botanist and geologist, in 1859. Hochstetter spent only a year here but contributed much, especially to the geological study of the country. The biggest of the moa was up to two metres at the shoulder and was represented in this upright stance in early drawings. It is now thought probable that the giant bird carried its head lower and further forward.

33

into more permanent communities, they still had an abundance of seafood to eat and rats and dogs, and became expert at snaring tree birds. But the days of the bonanza birds had gone by about the sixteenth century.

All this was of profound economic importance and signalled the introduction of Classic Maori culture. What evolved was pressure on resources among a growing population, together with claims for the best land along the most prolific seacoast or lakeside. Village life also changed from the late seventeenth and early eighteenth centuries. Hill forts (pa) proliferated. Doubts prevail that warfare or cannibalism was of serious consequence under the Archaic culture. It evolved with changing cultural mores caused by, or at least exacerbated by, inter-tribal competition for land. Even then, fighting was seasonal (not at kumara sowing or harvesting time), and was often ritual hand-to-hand combat with arms such as clubs (patu, mere) or the short fencing spear (taiaha). But inter-tribal bitterness actually peaked with the Musket Wars after Europeans arrived.

To understand fighting among tribes, think of the French and the English also competing in their world and so often at war over centuries. At the time of the Musket Wars in New Zealand, for example, war was endemic and almost continuous among European nations. Maori tribes saw themselves as separate, different nations. Whereas inter-tribal war once involved limited numbers of warriors, it began to expand on issues ·of territory as population grew – and *utu* ensured wars continued. Utu was about reciprocation, which included returns for favours, but more ominously it included revenge for insults, real or imagined, and developed in the way it did in Celtic societies (the Highland Scots, for example). The aftermath of a battle involved death and slavery for losers, and cannibalism – the eating of an enemy – was the greatest humiliation you could inflict. Thus the desire for utu among kinsmen of the defeated meant war never ended unless enemies and all their kin were extinguished.

Iwi, in the extreme isolation of this country, came to see it as the whole world, and each other as competing nations – Tainui against Te Arawa for example – even though they all had the same language with only slightly variant dialects. Hawaiiki – from whence they came and to which, in some traditions, they returned after death – was an empyrean place. Thus it's probable they had names for all the islands but no name for New Zealand as a country.

The nomenclature history is confusing, though. Although Tasman called his discovery *Staten Landt*, the name *Nova Zeelandia* appeared on Dutch charts from the 1640s, and Cook always referred to it as New Zealand once he had found it. So no ambivalence about that. But my generation was taught the romantic tale that when the mythical Polynesian explorer Kupe was approaching the country he saw the cloud that usually signalled land, and someone declared, 'Aotearoa', invariably translated then as 'Land of the Long White Cloud'. During the 1960s, the alternative and much more likely translation of 'long white day' or 'long white twilight' was postulated. Twilight in the summer would have impressed new arrivals from the tropics where day drops quickly into night.

Some indications are that Aotearoa was used early but for the North Island only, but *Te Iki a Maui*, the Fish of Maui, was a more common name for the North Island, consistent with the Maori myth of its origins. Historian Keith Sinclair said that in all the written Maori he had read from last century, 'Aotearoa' was used only once, in the 1870s, but he mentions *Tiritiri o te Moana* (the Gift of the Sea) as 'an ancient name for New Zealand'. Many Maori in the nineteenth century used *Nui Tirani*, a Maori transliteration of New Zealand, or *Nui Tireani*, as in *Te Karere o Nui Tirenii* (*The New Zealand Messenger*), a newspaper written in Maori and first published in 1842. Usage entrenched by William Pember Reeves's 1898 book, *The Long White Cloud: Ao Tea Roa*, and by James Cowan and other colonial writers has, nevertheless, given Aotearoa currency as the original Maori name for New Zealand.

Just as they probably had no name for the whole country, Maori had no name for themselves as a separate race of people because they knew of no other race. For the first few decades after the rediscovery, they were called 'natives' or 'New Zealanders' by the European newcomers. Eventually, they described themselves as 'Maori', a word for normal, usual, or ordinary, and the Europeans adopted it in the 1830s. Maori also adopted the word 'Pakeha' for non-Maori New Zealanders. Its derivation is unclear, although it was used as early as 1817. Harry Orsman's 1997 *Dictionary of New Zealand English* (Oxford University Press) says the 'least unlikely' of a number of suggested origins is 'pakepakeha' – which missionary and lexicographer Bishop William Williams defined in his 1844 dictionary as 'imaginary pale-skinned beings'.

Nomenclature confusion existed among Pakeha as well. They invested more significance in Stewart Island than it could eventually carry by calling the South Island 'Middle Island' until late in the nineteenth century.

But stories of grafting a living, of war and of cannibalism must not overshadow the creative imagination of the Maori who ornamented themselves, their artefacts and weapons, their canoes, their homes and the buildings on their marae (common ground) with objects of extraordinary beauty. The earliest settlers carved in a rectangular style but by the time of Classic Maori culture the style had moved toward spirals. No one has said it better than Sydney Parkinson, the artist who arrived in the *Endeavour* with Cook in 1769:

> The men have a particular taste for carving [with] a variety of flourishes, turnings and windings that are unbroken, but their favourite seems to be a volute, or spiral, which they vary many ways, single, double and triple, and with as much truth as if done from mathematical draughts: yet the only instruments we have seen are a chisel and an axe made of stone. Their fancy indeed is very wild and extravagant, and I have seen no imitations of nature

in any of their performances, unless the head and the heart-shaped tongue hanging out of the mouth, may be called natural.

Ornaments were also made from shell, bone and animal teeth and, the most coveted of all, from pounamu (greenstone). Pounamu came to have something of the same status in Maoridom as gold had in Europe. The value of its artefacts arose from their beauty and hardness and the rarity of the stone, and by the fact it was hard to work. Other stone tools were made by flaking but pounamu needed to be cut by toothed and abrasive saws made usually of sandstone.

Maori also carried in their oral culture a rich corpus of stories and beliefs which were first translated into English as fairy stories by non-literary Europeans. Their creation myth was as striking and imaginative as anyone else's and derivative of their Polynesian heritage. To simplify: their first ancestors were Rangi the sky father and Papa the earth mother, locked in a marital embrace. They produced sons – Tangaroa, the personification of the ocean and its inhabitants; Tawhiri of the weather; Tane of the forests and its inhabitants; indeed, a full Olympus of gods. Cramped for space and bereft of light, these gods forced their parents apart. Maori stories include the exploits of Maui, part man, part god, and all mischief, who was known throughout Polynesia. He fished up the North Island with the jawbone of his grandmother. Hence *Te Iki a Maui*.

Fundamental to all their beliefs was that Maori lived through their ancestors and their ancestors lived through them.

A wooden lintel carved during the Archaic Maori period, found near Kaitaia. The scroll and spiral ornamentation on the later Classic period is indigenously Maori without close similarity anywhere else in Polynesia.
(Trotter and McCulloch)

37

Chapter Four:

REDISCOVERY

NOT LONG AFTER Polynesians gave up long-haul sailing around the Pacific, the Europeans began it. In 1520, Portuguese navigator Ferdinand Magellan took his Spanish ship around Cape Horn and on around the world. Over the following centuries came more Spanish and Portuguese, then Dutch, English and French explorers. Trade, as they saw it, and exploitation as we see it looking back, was their motivation for exploration. They concentrated on commerce in the region we now call South-East Asia, mostly sailing around the Cape of Good Hope and up the east coast of Africa before striking eastward; or around Cape Horn and up the coast of South America, before striking westwards on the trade winds. Polynesia remained largely undisturbed but the geographical knowledge of the Pacific steadily grew.

During the early seventeenth century, plodding, largely incurious Dutch sea captains – called by the eminent New Zealand historian J. C. Beaglehole, 'plain men, ambitious for the most part only to bring their ships to port' – began fossicking around the edges of the known Pacific for overt signs of riches they could exploit. They got to know the coast of Australia better than others, and even sailed from the west across the Great Australian Bight, but they mostly saw desert and black people, and no sign of riches. The Great Barrier Reef kept them away from Australia's east coast.

European navigators did learn something of Polynesians,

though, as their ships brushed past the Tuamotus, and islands in the Tongan and Samoan groups.

Although the Dutch East India Company which controlled the Dutch traffic to the region was not given to non-commercial enterprises, it did send Tasman, accompanied by navigator Visscher, on his 1642–43 expedition to discover if the legendary southern continent existed. They found Tasmania, then the west coast of New Zealand and encountered Maori in what is now Golden Bay, but which they named Murderers' Bay. Tasman sent a ship's boat from the *Heemskerck* to the *Zeehaen*, with the warning not to accept aboard too many of the Maori paddling their canoes speedily around the ships. One of the canoes rammed the ship's boat and attacked its occupants. Four Dutch sailors were killed. Tasman fled.

Visscher suspected the presence of Cook Strait, probably from currents, but the the *Heemskerck* and *Zeehaen* sailed north up the west coast of the North Island. At the Three Kings Islands, which Tasman named, they sent boats to get fresh water, noting two canoes on the beach and cultivations, but did not risk landing because of the surf. They tried again

A Dutch expedition led by Abel Janszoon Tasman in the ships Heemskerck *and* Zeehaen *came upon the west coast of New Zealand in 1642 while searching for the legendary great southern continent. Four of his sailors were killed during a skirmish with Maori in what he called Murderers' Bay and has since been renamed Golden Bay, in the north-west of the South Island.*

This strange, static drawing of Maori in their canoe was found in Abel Tasman's journal.

39

the following day, reporting some 'giants' shouting at them from afar. So they never did land in New Zealand. They sailed north and found some islands in the Tongan and Fijian groups, and then returned to Batavia (now Jakarta, Indonesia). 'Zeelandia Nova' (or *Nova Zeelandia*) was put on the maps of the world by Dutch cartographers alongside a wiggly line showing a piece of the west coast of a land mass of unknown dimensions.

The name, in its anglicised form, stuck.

The Dutch showed no interest in following up Tasman's discoveries. But by the middle of the eighteenth century, the English and the French were both showing heightened interest in the Pacific. Royal Navy officer James Cook was despatched into the Pacific by the British government. He was to go to Tahiti to watch and measure the transit of Venus – one of many observations from around the world organised by the Royal Society to better measure the distance of the sun from the earth. After that it was his turn to search for the southern continent. Britain was the greatest maritime nation of the time, but the American colonies were getting restless and it was while Cook was at sea that the argument over taxation without representation took the violence there to a new level and presaged the American War of Independence.

Taken at sunset, this picture shows the statue of Captain James Cook on Kaiti Hill, Gisborne, looking out over the Pacific from the area first sighted by surgeon's boy Nicholas Young and named Young Nicks Head. Cook landed nearby and Maori were linked to the rest of the world.

Cook, a phlegmatic Yorkshireman, not only rediscovered New Zealand where Tasman (or more probably Visscher) had put his wiggly line, he went on to literally and meticulously place many Pacific countries on the map during three extensive voyages between 1768 and 1780. His second voyage (1772–75) was to explore the South Atlantic and the South Pacific, going as close to Antarctica as he could, continuing the search for a southern continent. His third expedition (1776–80) was to locate a short-cut, north-west passage from the Atlantic to the Pacific – which he didn't find either. But he did rediscover Hawaii.

The *Endeavour*'s first contact with New Zealand occurred on 6 October 1769, more than a year after she sailed from Plymouth. The surgeon's boy, Nicholas Young, up in the *Endeavour*'s masthead, sighted what became the eponymous Young Nicks Head in present-day Gisborne. From then, fairly quickly, for better or for worse, Maori joined the rest of the world.

A sturdy bark made for the coal trade, the *Endeavour* anchored in Poverty Bay. Cook landed and left the ship's boats in the care of some boys. When what may have been a ritual challenge by an armed Maori was understandably misread as a threat, one of the boys shot and killed the man. The next day, Cook landed with a party of marines and marched to a position on the beach carrying a Union Jack – which must have looked as bizarre to the Maori as the subsequent Maori haka did to the English. The Tahitian, Tupaia, discovered he and Maori could understand each other and he acted as interpreter. Next, Cook, courageously, advanced on one of the Maori. They saluted each other with a hongi (a touching of noses). But it all went wrong. Smart, practical Maori tried to grab the weapons being used so effectively against them and, indeed, one of them did get his hands on a sword. In the melee that followed four more were killed. Cook and his party went back to the ship with respect for the Maori as tough and brave, and saddened that some had been killed.

Romantics and myth-weavers won't leave it at that, though. Did others we don't know about find New Zealand? A metal helmet, usually referred to as 'the Spanish helmet' was 'discovered' in the National Museum in 1904, having been 'recovered', it was claimed, from Wellington Harbour. Any origin with an early, unidentified European expedition is discounted. A 'Tamil Bell' was identified as perhaps belonging to an Indian vessel that came this way. One story is that William Colenso discovered a group of Maori using it as a cooking pot, and markings on it were identified as of Tamil origin, suggesting a long-ago discovery by navigators from India. The claim has no verifiable credence. A Ngati Porou tradition and some obscure cartographic and other Spanish claims hint at a possible visit by a Spanish ship in the sixteenth century. While a Spanish or Portuguese landfall cannot be dismissed out of hand, any evidence is unexcitingly slender.

With each generation, new scientific techniques enlarge the information from the past. Kiore could only have reached New Zealand with man. Recent DNA studies at the University of Auckland suggest that ancient kiore came from several Pacific destinations, thus reinforcing the theory that a number of migrating expeditions arrived in this country. Sleuthing with DNA techniques and radio-carbon dating may yet provide a pattern of migration.

🐟 🐟 🐟

Sydney Parkinson, an artist on Cook's first voyage, drew this picture of a single-hulled Maori war canoe.

Aboard the *Endeavour* as supernumeraries on the first Cook expedition were English gentleman botanist Joseph Banks, Swedish botanist D. C. Solander and Scottish artist Sydney Parkinson. They recorded a wealth of information on the

plants, the animals and the people of the rediscovered countries. They agreed that Maori were slightly taller than the European average, fit, agile and industrious with the women markedly shorter. Older, grey-haired Maori were reported among the contacts. And yet modern archaeological pathology suggests their life expectancy was around the mid to late thirties – much the same as in England at that time. But Maori didn't suffer from malaria, measles, whooping cough, influenza, venereal diseases, dysentery – most of which the rediscoverers ultimately brought with them and which gradually decimated the local population. So what caused their early death in pre-European times? To the layman, the reasons seem inadequate. The main one was that fern root from which they received much of their carbohydrate was abrasive and wore their teeth to the gums when they were still young. This led to serious digestive problems. Evidence also from recovered skeletons suggests the hard life of shaping stone implements, working with wood to make houses and canoes, and carrying heavy loads, brought arthritis on early in their lives.

We know in detail what early visitors thought of Maori on first contact. Cook spent time at a number of places on the coast in 1769–70 when he, Banks and others made their freshest descriptions. His longest interface with any one group of Maori was in and around Ship Cove, Queen Charlotte Sound. He spent months there during three visits in 1770, 1773 and 1777, and his earliest reactions were positive – 'a brave, open and honest' people. During the second voyage, Cook consolidated his reputation for ably managing his crew and gaining the confidence, sometimes even the reverence, of Polynesians on the many islands, seldom resorting to violence.

His third voyage was very different. During the second voyage, his ship, the *Resolution*, had been parted from an accompanying vessel, the *Adventure*, skippered by Tobias Furneaux. When the *Adventure* arrived in Queen Charlotte Sound, a party from its less-disciplined crew was overcome during a skirmish with local Maori. When other *Adventure* crewmen went searching, they found their shipmates had been butchered and eaten at a cannibal feast. Cook didn't learn of this until long after he had left New Zealand on the return home. When he arrived early on the third voyage, he refused to punish the Maori even though he knew who was responsible. Thus he lost *mana* (or prestige) among Maori, who expected utu, and the respect of his crew, who were angry that he had not sought retribution for the horrible fate of their former colleagues.

No one can be sure whether this experience triggered Cook's personality change of the third voyage, or whether he was ill, or was exhausted at last from the strain of years at sea. The reigning contemporary authority on Cook, Dame Anne Salmond, thinks that the third was a voyage too far, cramped as he was for another year in the tiny wooden town of the ship; that he was worn out and suffered a crisis of command, increasingly disliked by his crew and seemingly disillusioned with Polynesians he had treated so astutely in the past. He certainly was a different man, uncharacteristically irascible and violent with both his crew and the islanders. His unpredictability contributed to his death at the hands of the Hawaiians.

If you read through the extensive literature, from Cook's journals through J. C. Beaglehole to Anne Salmond's *Two Worlds* and *Between Worlds*, the strong inference is that, putting cannibalism aside, the early British visitors admired Polynesians. They believed, of course, that the islanders were culturally and morally inferior, less civilised, but this was a reflexive British attitude at the time towards all 'natives', or 'Indians'. It was as though they couldn't help admiring especially the cheek of the Maori, their courage, curiosity, intelligence, humour, and their tough, practical approach to life with its Anglo-Saxon overtones. Although putting cannibalism aside was not easy because of the revulsion it provoked even among these life-hardened sailors.

Maori's earliest attitude to Pakeha was not documented, of course, but is not without witness. According to children who were there at the time, many years later, and according

'Man of New Zealand' was the name William Hodges gave to this picture in 1773 during Cook's second voyage.

to second-hand tales, the pale-skinned men in the huge ships were gods, or devils, or messengers from another world, given that Maori inhabited *this* whole world. Then, as one can guess, they saw them up close through the window of their own cultural behaviour – as everyone does – and thus with growing disenchantment. The visitors cut trees, caught fish, used the landscape as though it were theirs and, when they used the women as part of the trade for iron and cloth, it wasn't moral disapprobation they earned so much as contempt for leaving painful contagious venereal diseases behind. Maori respected the usefulness and power of muskets, swords, iron implements, nails, and literacy. And the missionaries told them the source of all power was a particular God reached through Jesus Christ.

※ ※ ※

Cook's circumnavigation and extraordinarily accurate charting of New Zealand in 1770 ended speculation that it was part of a continent. One effect his voyaging had on New Zealand was his opening up of the east coast of Australia, which the English government recognised as a potential repository for criminals. Transportation overseas had been a common punishment, and when newly independent American colonies became unavailable, New South Wales looked ideally remote.

The Colony of New South Wales was officially founded in 1788 under Governor Arthur Phillip. Sydney became the pivotal centre for the south-west Pacific. New Zealand was not a prospect for a penal settlement for a number of reasons, among them that the country was more densely populated and by a people much less tractable than indigenous Australians.

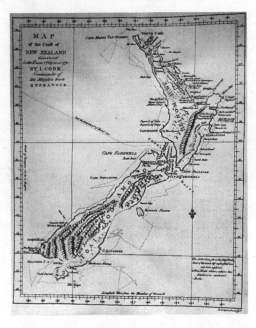

After arriving in New Zealand aboard the HMS Endeavour for his first visit in 1769, Cook circumnavigated New Zealand and drew this remarkably accurate chart, ending the belief that the west coast was the edge of a great southern continent. A sturdy bark, the Endeavour was made for the coal trade and proved a tough and stable vessel for the long, round-the-world journey.

45

Cook tells the story of his first encounter with Aborigines, in Botany Bay. Fishing parties took almost no notice of the *Endeavour* as she sailed close by, as though it was something beyond their experience and, therefore, not worthy of attention. A sharp contrast with inquisitive, aggressive Maori welcomes.

Chapter Five:

THE FORTUNE HUNTERS

NEW SOUTH WALES became a bustling colony, and within fifteen years of Cook's third and last visit, the extractive industries that dominated New Zealand's economy for many years began. A party of sealers was left in Dusky Sound to kill, skin and dress the animals' hides before being picked up in a few months' time. Hundreds of thousands of sealskins later, in the 1820s, the plunder of the New Zealand coast and the Subantarctic islands ended when the stock became so depleted the industry collapsed.

Whaling ships, mostly based in Sydney, began hunting the sperm whale for rendering down for its prized oil. But shore-based whaling soon took over. The first station opened on the shores of Tory Channel in 1829 and the last of more than a hundred of them was closed in 1964 by Gilbert Perano, whose family had been whaling in the Cook Strait area since 1911.

Cook had noted on his first visit how tall and straight was the kauri and how high its lowest branches: ideal for ships' spars. The Royal Navy began cutting in the Thames district at the mouth of the Waihou River before the end of the eighteenth century. The industry spread north to the Bay of Islands and the Hokianga where the small town of Horeke became a timber and shipbuilding centre. Kauri gum, the congealed sap of the great trees, found under the ground and used for manufacturing polishes, became a major Northland

Phormium tenax, the New Zealand flax, was quickly recognised as economically of high value for cordage and as a packaging material. Maori women were involved in treating and plaiting flax until demand lifted to the level where machinery was developed. In places like Foxton, near the outlet of the Manawatu River, the industry remained profitable until the artificial fibres of the mid-twentieth century took over.

industry. Flax was an early export. Indeed, cordage from *Phormium tenax* was so valued the industry continued as an earner until the artificial fibres of the twentieth century supplanted it.

Life below decks in the sealers and whalers was squalid, cramped and miserable beyond the modern imagination. Sealing teams left in Westland or on the Bounty or Auckland Islands lived in circumstances of unremitting deprivation as they waited, often through winter months, for their ships to return without knowing when or even, in some cases, if they would. Captains were often ruthless men who used their authoritarian power to abuse crews in a variety of ways, especially with floggings. They took on Maori and other Polynesian sailors and frequently landed them on alien shores without pay. To work in this environment, seamen were for the most part ruffians and for the least part adventurers looking to make their fortune in the new countries of the south-west Pacific.

Maori were involved in the early industries, especially timber and shipbuilding and flax processing. Their lives had changed quickly and in so many ways, including the clothes they wore and the food they ate. English plants and pastoral animals were immediately at home in New Zealand's temperate climate – in many cases more so than in England. The potato grew faster than the kumara and throughout most of the year.

🌿 🌿 🌿

Hard on the heels of the sealers, whalers and coastal traders came the Anglican missionaries under the auspices of the rich and redoubtable Samuel Marsden, chaplain to the New South Wales colony. Marsden was a stern wielder of the lash among the convicts but had become an admirer of Maori, initially from his acquaintance with visitors to Sydney. He persuaded the Anglican Church Missionary Society (CMS) in London to start a mission in the Bay of Islands, despite the general depiction of Maori as fierce and fractious.

The first missionaries would have arrived in 1809 but for a massacre which unnerved the two who were poised in Sydney to come over: English-trained William Hall and John King. The flogging of a young Maori chief provoked utu when most of the crew and passengers of the vessel *Boyd* were killed by local Maori at Whangaroa, persuading an uncomprehending world to steer clear of a country in which such savagery prevailed.

History has perhaps been unkind to the CMS men and women who came here. They squabbled excessively but compared with, say, the severe puritans in Hawaii, New Zealand was host to a group relatively light on cultural oppression. Marsden believed the path to Christ for Maori was paved with hard work in the practical pursuit of British-style agriculture, mechanics and commerce, leading to his version of 'moral and industrious habits'. The missionaries were men trained in such arts as carpentry, shipbuilding, shoe-making, rope-making and printing, but not all so well trained in evangelism.

The first mission station was at Rangihoua, home of Marsden's friend, Maori chief Ruatara. Hall, King and Thomas Kendall, an English-trained schoolteacher, arrived in the country with Marsden late in 1814 aboard the *Active*

Whalers and sealers were in New Zealand waters in numbers from within twenty years of Captain Cook's first voyage. This illustration by W. M. Davis is called Nimrod of the Sea, *showing longboat crewmen in the prows of their vessels ready to launch their harpoons into the whale. The ship is flying an American flag. American whalers in the Pacific outnumbered those from any other nation, even in the coastal waters around New Zealand.*

Accompanied by missionaries, the redoubtable Reverend Samuel Marsden arrived in the Bay of Islands from Sydney in 1814 to set up an Anglican Church Missionary Society station. Marsden brought a variety of plants and livestock, including the first cattle, and his aim was to encourage 'moral and industrious habits' among Maori.

– along with a variety of plants and livestock, including New Zealand's first cattle. Marsden preached New Zealand's first Christian service on Christmas Day, with a touch of salesmanship: 'Behold I bring you tidings of great joy', from St Luke.

This took place six months before the Battle of Waterloo on the other side of the world.

Ruatara had been to England, spent much time on British ships, lived and worked for some years in Sydney with Marsden, and was the most cosmopolitan Maori of his time, the one who best bestrode the two cultures. His death early the following year was a serious setback for the mission. The most interesting of the early arrivals was Kendall who was bewitched by Maori and their mores and beliefs. He was disgraced by sleeping with a Maori woman.

The missionaries were the first group to move inland, with most traders keeping to coastal towns and villages. Most of them learnt Maori and were influential in putting the language into writing. Marsden began a vocabulary, and Kendall published a Maori dictionary in 1815. Five years later, Kendall went to England with a famed Ngapuhi chief Hongi Hika and his kinsman Waikato and together they helped a Cambridge linguist, Samuel Lee, put together *Grammar and Vocabulary of the New Zealand Language*. Soon afterwards, CMS missionary-printer William Colenso translated and printed the New Testament and other books. Maori quickly understood the power of writing and a surprising number of them became literate in the early years.

The missionaries found Maori had a complex and profound religion themselves, one that answered in its own way many of the spiritual needs Christians claimed they alone satisfied. When Maori did begin to convert to Christianity in numbers from the late 1830s, they were especially attracted to the Old Testament, which some of their leaders adapted to support cults of their own.

The first Methodists came in 1823 and French Catholic Bishop Pompallier, a man of important religious and political influence, arrived in the Hokianga in 1838.

If the missionaries were doing God's work, rum and dangerous locally distilled drinks imbibed by the flotsam of the whaling and sealing business were doing the devil's work at Kororareka, one of the Pacific's most lawless towns. Lawless is the precise word because New Zealand was an independent state that belonged to no one except Maori, whose government was minutely fragmented. Chiefs controlled small regions, often precariously in the face of possible attacks from neighbours. Cook may have traipsed up hills around the country to stick a flag into the ground and claim the country for England's King, but no one followed it up. The missionaries were guests of local chiefs, and, during the continuing rivalries and local wars, areas of the country were powder-kegs.

The French Catholic missionary, Bishop Pompallier, arrived in the Hokianga in 1838 and became an important political and religious influence in New Zealand in the early years of Pakeha settlement.

Hongi Hika was first off in what became known as the Musket Wars. When he went to England with Kendall he became a social lion, and was given many gifts. Before he left New Zealand, he had already used muskets to attack the Ngati Porou of the East Coast. On his way home from England, he traded his gifts for more muskets and over the next ten years rampaged through the North Island killing and enslaving hundreds of enemy. Soon other tribes were trading food for muskets, and fighting chiefs such as Kawiti, Patuone, Waka Nene, Te Wherowhero and, further south, Te Rauparaha, set the country alight. It was a sad period for Maori already suffering from introduced diseases. War-weariness was a factor in their acquiescence when the British annexed the country in 1840.

Meanwhile, adventurous traders like Sydney-born Johnny Jones, and Englishmen William Barnard Rhodes and Edward Weller, all with business interests in Australia, saw the potential for making money here. Jones and Rhodes came on whaling expeditions and Weller to set up a whaling shore station. They realised the South Island, especially its

51

Sydney-born Johnny Jones was one of a number of adventurous traders who saw commercial possibilities in New Zealand. He worked his way up from crewman on a whaler to a ship's owner, sponsored a settlement at Riverton in Southland, and created a farm at Waikouaiti in Otago. Something of a freebooter, Jones ultimately gained a kind of respectability and became a successful entrepreneur in Dunedin with substantial shipping interests.

deforested east coast, would be ideal for pastoral farming. They bought hundreds of thousands of hectares. Jones, Rhodes and Weller and men like them were freebooters in their own jurisdiction rather than gentlemen pioneers, traders or farmers, although Jones and Rhodes ultimately gained a kind of respectability.

Jones worked his way up from the crew of a whaling ship to owner, bought large tracts of land in the South Island in the 1830s and tried to persuade chiefs not to sign the Treaty of Waitangi because he guessed, correctly, that his purchases wouldn't stand too diligent a scrutiny. Part ruffian, part businessman, he sponsored a whaling station at Riverton, in Southland, the oldest European settlement in the South Island. He later built up a farm in Waikouaiti, near Oamaru, and eventually became a successful entrepreneur in Dunedin with substantial shipping interests.

Rhodes, a tough, mean man, had also skippered a whaling ship and acquired large landholdings which he managed from Wellington in partnership with younger brothers. When he died in 1878 he was probably New Zealand's richest man, leaving more than four million pounds.

Weller was a trader on Otago Harbour who successively married two Maori women and made huge land claims before moving back to Australia.

Some Europeans in the Bay of Islands and the Hokianga, including the missionaries, stayed on here and put down the roots of families that flourish today. Some few Pakeha Maoris, as they were known, attached themselves to tribes and took Maori wives.

❦ ❦ ❦

By 1840, exports had more than doubled over less than a decade, mainly through Kororareka, the country's first capital. The national Pakeha population had reached 2000, significant numbers of Maori were converting to Christianity, and the French were sniffing around. France's Jean François Marie de Surville was off the coast within days of Cook's first

Left: *Self-styled Baron de Thierry, English-born of French parents, anointed himself King of New Zealand in 1837 and tried to buy land and set up his kingdom in the North Island. An eccentric, he was the centrepiece of a novel,* Check to Your King, *by Robin Hyde.*

Right: *The Colonial Office in London appointed James Busby as British Resident. He had no army, no navy, no police, not even a right of arrest. Based in the Bay of Islands, his task was to persuade the Europeans to behave themselves and the Maori to set up some sort of coherent government. Busby was the country's first viticulturist.*

arrival, but neither he nor Marion du Fresne a few years later stayed very long, nor managed to establish any kind of rapport with Maori. Dumont d'Urville in 1827 in the *Astrolabe* stayed longer and charted French Pass. In 1837, a deluded, self-styled Baron de Thierry, English-born of French parents, anointed himself King of New Zealand. Perhaps his greatest legacy is his bizarre life as told in a novel, *Check to Your King*, by Robin Hyde.

Given all this instability, the missionaries and those settlers who had established themselves tried to persuade the British government that Maori needed protection. The first response was the appointment by the Colonial Office of James Busby. Poor old Busby was a keen viticulturist with limited public service experience whom nobody seemed to like much. He was British Resident of an independent territory with no army, no navy, no police, no right of arrest even, just a man on his own trying to persuade Pakeha to be good and Maori to set up some form of national government. Given those conditions, he didn't do too badly. In 1835, he organised a Declaration of the Independence of New Zealand, signed eventually by fifty-two chiefs. It declared an independent Maori state, pledged friendship and protection for British citizens, and asked King William IV to be parent and protector (which he agreed to). This led to a Confederation of United Tribes, complete with its own flag.

Events were closing in, however, and making a Maori-governed nation less and less likely. Industrial activity was expanding, settlers organised by the New Zealand Company in England were on the way, land sales were being transacted with Maori in a haphazard way between rapacious buyers and sellers who didn't understand the concept of individual land title – all this in a country without government. Colonists, missionaries and New Zealand, Australian and British businessmen sought formal British intervention to impose law and order where a dangerous muddle prevailed. The British government vacillated. It could foresee – accurately over the following thirty years as it turned out – more expense in imposing law and order than it could foresee profit from trade or tax.

A profound change in social attitudes had occurred in England since the penal colony had been set up in New South Wales fifty years before. The British government was feeling good about itself after abolishing slavery throughout the empire in 1834 as a result of the drive of Christian philanthropist William Wilberforce and others. It was also aware of what was happening to the Australian Aborigines who were being shot out in parts of Australia. It wanted to do the right thing by Maori. However, accelerating, organised British settlement pressed hard on these ideals. As historian Claudia Orange puts it: 'By 1839 the Colonial Office was no longer contemplating, as they had previously, a Maori New Zealand in which settlers had somehow to be accommodated, but a settler New Zealand in which a place had to be kept for Maori.'

Later the original ideals became shadows almost obliterated by the encroachment of settlers on Maori land and rights.

In January 1840, Captain William Hobson arrived in the Bay of Islands and announced he was Lieutenant-Governor of New Zealand, responsible to the Governor of New South Wales. He knew that getting Maori acceptance of British sovereignty was critical. Hence, a week later, came the Treaty of Waitangi and all it has meant for New Zealand since.

On May 21, Hobson proclaimed British sovereignty over the whole country. The French were very interested in the Pacific and assiduously exploring it. French 'scares' led to the precipitous founding of British colonies (some of them penal) in Tasmania, Victoria, Western Australia and Northern Territory, and it was a rumour of French interest that induced Britain to claim the Cook Islands as a protectorate as late as 1888.

Back in July 1840, a French corvette had arrived in the Bay of Islands, and the Lieutenant-Governor knew of a plan for a French settlement on Banks Peninsula. He decided to send a ship, HMS *Britomart* post-haste to occupy the area and hoist the Union Jack. This was recounted later as a race between the British and the French to claim the South Island but, given the nationality of most of the settlers in the country, the French would have been foolhardy to have contested British sovereignty. The French migrants arrived shortly afterwards, and established an exotic enclave in Akaroa. They became British citizens.

In November 1840 – with the Treaty of Waitangi signed by as many chiefs around the country as could be persuaded to do so – Hobson became Governor and New Zealand a separate Crown Colony.

Chapter Six:

THE TREATY AND
ITS CONSEQUENCES

William Hobson arrived at the Bay of Islands with notes made from instructions issued by Lord Normanby, Colonial Secretary in London, and he and James Busby cobbled together the English version of the Treaty of Waitangi in just a few days. It was translated into Maori and on February 6, 1840, many Bay of Islands chiefs signed up. How much they understood remains unclear.

T HE TREATY OF WAITANGI – an original in the annals of European colonisation which has reverberated throughout our history – was cobbled together in a few days, mainly by James Busby from notes by William Hobson and his staff. Hobson's notes were, in turn, based on instructions from the Colonial Secretary in London, Lord Normanby. That was the English version. Then it was translated into Maori overnight by the leader of the CMS mission since 1823, Henry Williams, and his 21-year-old son before it had to be 'sold' next day, 5 February 1840, to a big gathering of Maori – more than 500 of them. And sold it was.

Because the British government had acknowledged Maori sovereignty in the Declaration of Independence five years before, a signed treaty was critical for a legitimate annexation. Hobson knew that if Maori walked away, annexation would have become seriously difficult; so the explanations on the day of what the hastily prepared text meant were, well, sugared, stressing the advantages of signing.

The first Maori speakers went against the Treaty and the prospects for getting signatures that mattered looked slim. Bishop Pompallier arrived, seeking an assurance that religious freedom would be allowed, and got one from Hobson. Some Maori chiefs challenged the missionaries and Busby to give back the land they had already bought. Although Hone Heke, Patuone and Tamati Waka Nene spoke in favour of signing, it was clear the matter wasn't going to be resolved that day.

The next meeting was scheduled for two days later but the assembled Maori were getting impatient and talked the issue over during the night. On 6 February, they wanted another meeting. Heke was invited to sign, and he did, followed by most of the others, almost all of them from the Bay of Islands. The Treaty then went to Horeke in the Hokianga and on around the country for more than 500 chiefs to sign; but leaders of Waikato, Ngati Maniapoto, Arawa and some other important tribes were not among them. In May, Hobson asserted British sovereignty separately over both the North Island and the South Island. The two major islands becoming separate colonies was briefly a possibility.

The Treaty was an original because it formally acknowledged that an indigenous people had rights. However, over the years, Pakeha, few of whom ever bothered to read it, thought it simply signalled Maori acceptance of British citizenship and sovereignty and made us 'one people', an absurd, surreal phrase Hobson kept mumbling in Maori as each chief signed at Waitangi. The Treaty may have married two races but like all hasty unions it has given both parties

Leader of the Church Missionary Society in New Zealand since 1823, Henry Williams, with help from his 21-year-old son, translated the English version of the Treaty of Waitangi into Maori overnight. Scholars in recent years have questioned whether the translation was as accurate as it should have been.

Perhaps the most historic building in the country, the house that New Zealand Resident James Busby built at Waitangi in 1834, seen here as it was at the time of the New Zealand centenary celebrations in 1940. The house was the meeting place for negotiators leading up to the signing of the Treaty in 1840. It was privately owned until the Waitangi Estate came up for sale in 1931. The Governor-General, Viscount Bledisloe, bought it and presented it to the people of New Zealand.

much leisure for repentance. More people of both races in the present generation know the details of the Treaty than at any previous time.

Like Busby's Declaration of Independence a few years before, the Treaty is not written in the inspirational prose of the American equivalent. Neither Busby nor Hobson was a Thomas Jefferson, who would himself have been stretched to turn the document into ringing rhetoric, given the time allowed. And Hobson wasn't well. He died two years later.

What surprises most people when they read the Treaty for the first time is its brevity – a preamble of about 200 words, followed by three articles, and wound up with another hundred or so words in which the signatories say they understand what it means.

With the first article in the English version, the chiefs cede to the Queen 'absolutely and without reservation all the rights and powers of Sovereignty' over their respective territories.

With the second, the Queen 'confirms and guarantees to the Chiefs and Tribes of New Zealand and to the respective families and individuals thereof the full exclusive and undisturbed possession of their Lands and Estates Forests Fisheries and other properties which they may collectively or individually possess so long as it is their wish and desire to retain the same in their possession'; but the chiefs 'yield to Her Majesty the exclusive right of Preemption over such lands as the proprietors thereof may be disposed to alienate at such prices as may be agreed upon between the respective Proprietors and persons appointed by Her Majesty to treat with them in that behalf'.

With the third, the Queen 'extends to the Natives of New Zealand Her royal protection and imparts to them all the Rights and Privileges of British Subjects'.

Big questions hang over the Williams's Maori translation, the version that Maori studied on the day. How much they understood is endlessly debatable. As the first chiefs went to sign, William Colenso sought assurance that they knew the full ramifications. That he did this in front of his superiors, Hobson, Williams and other officials, suggests deep concern. One chief said famously afterwards that the Treaty meant 'the shadow of the land goes to Queen Victoria, but the substance remains with us'. An unreal understanding of its meaning can be inferred from that statement. But no matter how you read either version, no doubt can exist that Maori were offered more than they got.

Dr Arthur S. Thomson, surgeon-major to the 58th Regiment of the British Army, spent eleven years in New Zealand, and in 1859 wrote in his *The Story of New Zealand* (the first substantial history): 'Few natives rightly comprehended the nature of the treaty . . .' The 58th arrived from Sydney in 1845 to help curb rebellion by the once-compliant Treaty signatory Hone Heke. Thomson said the Treaty 'did this great good to the New Zealanders and to the cause of peace; it clearly recognised their legal title to all the land in the country, and on that account the act may be denominated the Magna Carta of the people'.

That was written on the eve of the big campaigns of the New Zealand Wars.

Rumblings of dissatisfaction among Maori never abated but they had been sidelined as a culture by the end of the nineteenth century. Pakeha diseases ravaged them. Tuberculosis remained a scourge until the disease itself was subdued in the 1960s. Most Maori lived in rural areas until after World War II and many of their political leaders succumbed to Pakeha assumptions about the Treaty. Sir Apirana Ngata wrote a condescending explanation for 'a dear old lady' in 1922:

Sir Apirana Ngata, in a 1922 letter to 'a dear old lady', seemed to capitulate to Pakeha thinking on the meaning of the Treaty, claiming Maori had violated the authority of the 'Queen of England' and land was taken in payment.

The Government placed in the hands of the Queen of England the sovereignty and the authority to make laws. Some sections of the Maori people violated that authority. War arose from this and blood was spilled. The law came into operation and the land was taken in payment. This in itself was a Maori custom – revenge, plunder to avenge a wrong. It was their own chiefs who ceded that right to the Queen. The confiscations cannot therefore be objected to in the light of the treaty . . .

This was an extraordinary capitulation to Pakeha thinking.

✿ ✿ ✿

What historians have written over the years tells us much about what their contemporaries were thinking when the various accounts were given. Generations of New Zealand schoolchildren were taught about a benign Britain spreading moral and social enlightenment around a grateful empire. The inference was we should revel in our luck, acknowledge our gratitude. Maori were always perplexed that the Treaty of Waitangi hadn't worked out for them as they had hoped, but Pakeha were looking at a rose-tinted past, congratulating Britain and themselves for their competent, compassionate and generous governance of two races as one people. In fact, our own national story was relegated to the margins of formal education which was dedicated almost entirely to the history of glorious Britain.

Between 1945 and 1950, A. H. Reed's *The Story of New Zealand* sold an extraordinary (for that time) 12,000 copies, including a school edition of 2600 in 1948, when I was being taught history at Wellington College. Reed was an honest,

A. H. Reed's best-selling The Story of New Zealand *in the late 1940s was a sentimental, Anglo-centric account of Maori-Pakeha relations that reflected public attitudes of the time. Reed was born in England and came to New Zealand with his parents in 1887. He worked as a gum-digger and became a bookseller in Dunedin. His firm of A. H. and A. W. Reed began publishing in 1932 and was the major publishing house for many years. Reed wrote many provincial histories and became famous as a prodigious walker before his death at age ninety-nine. He climbed Mt Egmont at eighty, Ruapehu at eighty-three and Ngauruhoe at eighty-five.*

decent man in everything he did, but as a historian he was imprisoned in the conventional thinking of his time. His account of the preparation and signing of the Treaty of Waitangi was written in a sentimental glow. It implies the argument between Maori who wanted to sign and those who did not was, on 5 February 1840, between the good guys and the bad. He wrote: 'It was clear that (the signing of the Treaty) was high time for the coming of British law and justice.' In stumbling prose, he continued: 'According to the Maori code, the British being the stronger, they would have been quite justified in taking the country by conquest, and driving out those who had themselves driven out the Morioris. No one doubts that Britain could have done it . . .'

Reed did not appreciate the very serious doubts whether the British government could have afforded the moral or material resources it would have taken to 'conquer' Maori in 1840. Twenty years later with thousands more colonists and a relatively developed infrastructure, the British Army and colonists found it extremely difficult and costly to quell fragmented Maori rebellions. And throughout the early pioneering period Pakeha were still dependent on Maori for food.

I was taught at school that mighty Great Britain had been entirely altruistic in offering the Treaty, that agricultural and industrial development led from this, and that the Treaty had worked benignly for Maori whose gratitude explained why our race relations were exemplary. Where I lived, we never heard the rumblings that apparently never ceased in Maori communities.

This pretty picture of our country fell off the wall in 1959 with the publication of Keith Sinclair's A *History of New Zealand*, a seminal book that was still in print at the end of the century. For the first time, New Zealand history was seen through the clear, cool eye of a scholar. After that, even the nomenclature began to change. The pejorative Maori Wars became the Land Wars, then the New Zealand Wars; and may perhaps

Keith Sinclair's A History of New Zealand was published in 1959 and became the standard popular work for more than forty years. It was the first look at the New Zealand story through the cool, clear eyes of a scholar, unclouded by the sentimentality of previous popular historians. Professor of History at the University of Auckland, Sinclair was also a biographer and poet.

one day become the New Zealand Civil War, considering Maori were, all along, British citizens.

More lately still, the Treaties of Waitangi – both the English and Maori renditions – have been semantically picked over thoroughly by scholars. Are they quite the same document? A point at issue is whether the Maori words and phrases used for 'sovereign authority' and 'civil government' conveyed their meaning in such a way that Maori could reasonably have been expected to understand. Historian Claudia Orange notes these and other differences in the two versions and even hints at her belief that Henry Williams was not innocent of deceit in his translation.

The thirty years from the signing of the Treaty were turbulent as the transformation of New Zealand began to take place from a land of forests and deep bush to a pastoral replica of Britain. A review of land deals that were made before the Treaty was signed invalidated many of the most extravagant. But a new frenzy of land buying by settlers – and selling by Maori – began as soon as New Zealand Company settlers arrived from Britain in 1839. These transactions were complicated by obscure notions of who had title – which chiefs of which areas, and whether chiefs had rights over land which had traditionally been communally held by members of hapu.

With few Maori living in the south, virtually the whole of the South Island passed to the government. Millions of acres shifted into the settlers' hands in the North Island, much faster than they could make use of it. The first Attorney-General, William Swainson, claimed that on the eve of the Taranaki War when settlers were hungry for more land, they had not cultivated more than 43,000 acres of 130,000 already in their possession. And ownership of this particular area contained the seeds of conflict to come.

As early as 1843, a dispute over who owned which land resulted in what was coined the 'Wairau Massacre' by angry

Nelson settlers and for many years the general public, even though quite soon after the event objective observers realised the settlers had been pushing their luck. The later, fairer, revisionist term is 'Wairau Affray'. Captain Arthur Wakefield of the famous New Zealand Company family and a group of Nelson settlers attempted to arrest chiefs Te Rauparaha and Te Rangihaeata for resisting a survey of disputed land. Their attitude carried implied superior rights. A settler, it was claimed, fired a shot during a stand-off and a short, sharp skirmish ensued during which nine Maori and twenty-two settlers were killed, some after surrendering.

Disillusioned Ngapuhi Treaty signatories Hone Heke and Kawiti rebelled in the north in 1845. They had a range of motives including a loss of trading opportunities with the movement of the capital from Kororareka to Auckland, and the issues of chiefly control within their region. Other Ngapuhi, notably a faction led by Tamati Waka Nene, opposed them. Heke cut down the flagpole at Kororareka four times and sacked the town – but only after the population had fled. He fought only soldiers, not civilians, because he didn't want to drive Pakeha out given the trading advantages of their presence. A series of battles ensued in which, for the first time, substantial British forces were engaged against Maori. They were badly beaten by a smaller force led by Kawiti at Ohaeawai. The rebellion ended after Kawiti and about 500 followers defended the famous Ruapekapeka pa near Kawakawa against a force of about 1500, one-third of them Maori, backed by heavy artillery. The campaign was important because, according to historian James Belich, it convinced Maori that defending their evolving, well-engineered pa was the best way to win battles against superior British numbers.

Hone Heke was the first Maori leader to sign the Treaty of Waitangi, but became disillusioned and famously cut down the flagstaff near Kororareka four times. He also sacked the town and joined fellow Ngapuhi chief Kawiti in open rebellion. They inflicted a serious loss on British forces at Ohaewai but were subdued by a larger force after the battle of Ruapekapeka. Heke's motives in rebelling were complex but included loss of trading opportunities with the shift of the capital from Kororareka to Auckland and a loss of chiefly control in his region.

During the fifteen years after the rebellion in the north, serious clashes over land broke out between Maori and Pakeha in Wellington and Wanganui, and pressure began to

63

build up in Taranaki, including tension between Maori who wanted to sell land and those who didn't. These three places were sites of New Zealand Company settlements in which colonists were pressing for room to expand.

From the early 1850s, the attitude of many Maori leaders was hardening against land sales as they watched Pakeha settlements spread out from their townships. Also, they saw their chiefly authority diminished, brushed aside by Pakeha officialdom. This also gave impetus to the idea of some form of self-government.

In 1858, Potatau Te Wherowhero was made Maori King with support from the Ngati Maniapoto, Ngati Haua, and some hapu in Waikato, Taupo, East Coast and Hawke's Bay. The movement was consolidating control over a region in which their Maori tribal law had always prevailed, even since the arrival of Pakeha. The dynasty continues today.

It was in 1858, too, that the Pakeha population, at around sixty thousand, passed the declining estimated number of Maori.

Chapter Seven:

THE NEW ZEALAND WARS

THE MAJOR CAMPAIGNS of the New Zealand Wars began in 1860 over the sale forced by the government of a block of Maori land at Waitara. The Governor, Thomas Gore Browne, told a meeting in Taranaki he would never condone the sale of land with disputed title, but neither would he tolerate interference in a sale by Maori with no legitimate claim to it. A Waitara man, Te Teira, stood up and offered for sale a block of which he claimed ownership. The senior chief at Waitara, Wiremu Kingi, said the land was owned by the people and not just by Te Teira's group. As senior chief, he said: 'I will not give it up, I will not, I will not, I will not. I have spoken.' Kingi and his followers then walked out. Over a period of some months, the government and its local land buyer – wrongly as the government later, too late, admitted – decided the land belonged to Te Teira and bought it from him.

By the 1850s, a number of Maori farming enterprises were flourishing. The Waikato tribes were trading their fruit, vegetables and grains. The Ngati Raukawa were successfully growing fruit, vegetables and wheat and milking cows around Otaki. Maori at Motueka had 1000 acres in wheat and 600 in other produce. At Waitara, Wiremu Kingi's people were reported to be wealthy in terms of cash, with a 150 horses, 300 head of cattle, and ploughs and harrows and sailing boats to transport their produce for sale. In many

Governor Thomas Gore Browne said he would never condone the sale of land at Waitara with disputed title – but then did just that on the advice of a local land buyer. It was the spark that ignited the war in Taranaki. The deal not only provoked Maori to fight, it made an implacable enemy of Wiremu Kingi, previously a friend to Pakeha.
(Alexander Turnbull Library, F-71666-1/2)

65

places, Maori were more successful farmers than the settlers, with their nuclear families, because of readily available tribal labour which worked on a subsistence basis. This didn't endear them to the Pakeha.

But the more you read about the tensions that developed, the more strongly you sense that humiliation, a denigration of Maori chieftainship, was at least a component of all the disputes. Maori believed the Treaty had offered more influence over their affairs than they had. The government and the colonists were unremitting in the imposition of the British right to rule – to civilise the Natives, as they saw it. This was consistent with their attitude throughout the Empire to what they regarded as subject races. Maori generally remained remote from government interference, help or the bestowal of rights. Swainson, a sturdy supporter all his life of the Treaty of Waitangi as a protection for Maori, wrote after war broke out in Taranaki:

> In terms at least the New Zealand Constitution makes no distinction of race. The Natives are acknowledged to be the owners of the soil – to have, in fact, a right of proprietorship like landlords of estates; but it has been denied that they have such an interest in it under the Native tenure as to entitle them, within the meaning of the Act, to vote at the election. In return for their cession of the sovereignty, we have undertaken to impart to them the rights and privileges of British subjects. Yet we have given them no voice in the Government of the country, while we tax them for its support.

Thus the causes of the wars were more complex than simply the fight for land, although that became the focus. Land was at once tangible and a symbol as it had been for Hone Heke and Kawiti. Later, at Orakau, the defenders chanted an ancestral adage in Maori during the preparations and during the battle: 'The warrior's death is to die for the land.'

When government surveyors moved onto the Waitara land the government had bought from Te Teira, Maori women began obstructing the work. Gore Browne declared martial law. Troops moved in and destroyed the homes of Wiremu

Kingi and his people. If any doubt had existed among Maori about whether their land was at risk from official seizure, it was dispelled. Kingi, a former ally of the government in earlier disputes, a man who had refused to join the King Movement with its intractable attitude toward land sales, now reached out to King Potatau.

Warriors from the Kingite tribes went to Taranaki to help Kingi and, for a time, they humbled the British regulars and the settlers' forces. Settlers' properties were ransacked and New Plymouth remained under threat for months as Maori war parties pressed against its constricting perimeter. Women and children were evacuated to Nelson. But in 1861, British regulars – at one time 10,000 were in the country – had some successes, and after a period of stalemate a truce was called by George Grey, Governor from 1845 to 1853, who had returned from administering Cape Colony in South Africa to succeed Gore Browne for another term as governor.

The war shifted to the Waikato, Bay of Plenty and northern King Country. Grey, characteristically, assumed as much power as he could but an elected colonial government had more control than anyone in the country had held over him previously. He supported land acquisition on the one hand but he and the Premier William Fox also proposed that Maori districts should have self-government with rununga, or district councils, with the power to adopt by-laws with the approval of the governor on fencing, cattle trespassing, the sale of spirits and other prescribed matters. Each region was to have a European civil commissioner, resident magistrate and doctors, but with Maori police, teachers, assessors, jurors and their own prisons. Some few districts had had resident magistrates since the 1840s but colonists were wary of any extension of Maori power or any intrusion into law-making.

The proposals may have mollified chiefly concerns about influence, and given them a sense of control over their land

– but they were ten years too late. The Waikato War had become inevitable. Land-hungry settlers and businessmen in Auckland had their eyes on the rich land to the south.

Grey was preparing for war, and rumours of imminent Maori rebellion abounded in Auckland, where they feared an attack on the town. The government set up a line of settlements of ex-soldier pensioners stretching across the isthmus to the south of the town, from Howick to Onehunga.

Grey extended a road towards the Waikato, which further exacerbated Maori assumptions that an assault was to be made on their land. He then used British Army units under General Cameron to invade, ostensibly to punish Kingites for supporting Wiremu Kingi in Taranaki, but more likely to impose sovereignty on dissidents. The British were professional soldiers, well organised and with solid logistical support. Maori were part-time warriors whose support in war was necessarily based on subsistence, and who had to return to their homes at planting and harvesting time.

The Waikato War opened with bush skirmishes but in the end was resolved by set-piece battles: Maori building pa and defending them against attack. Some Kingite chiefs had been reluctant to fight, but because the alternative was unconditional surrender to the advancing army, they saw it as the only way to maintain a place in the world.

British Army General Cameron led the invasion of the Waikato, using gunboats on the Waikato River and winning a Pyrrhic victory at Rangiriri before moving south and east into flourishing tribal lands.

General Cameron used gunboats on the Waikato River to outflank Maori and shell their defences as well as to keep his supplies coming as he extended his drive south. He conquered a pa at Mercer and moved up the river to Rangiriri, where he scored a Pyrrhic victory, losing 132 killed or wounded compared with about half that by the Maori, some of whom escaped and some of whom expected to parley after raising a white flag – but were then captured.

The Kingites didn't bother to defend their headquarters at Ngaruawahia, preferring to fall back to protect their agricultural base in central and southern Waikato. They built a series of defensive pa, one of them at Orakau, a village near Kihikihi, not far from Te Awamutu. Under the direction of a CMS missionary, John Morgan, Maniapoto and other related tribes had turned this part of southern Waikato into a food bowl with hundreds of acres of wheat, a flour mill, large vegetable gardens, peach and apple orchards and livestock. Indeed the pa was built in a peach grove. No one could accuse them of not using the land productively. But all the time, Morgan was a spy, regularly sending the civil authorities information on the Kingites.

The pa was still incomplete when Brigadier-General Carey attacked with about 1200 troops on 31 March 1864. Reinforcements soon swelled the force to about 1700 and General Cameron arrived halfway through the fight. About 300 Maori, including women and children, under the leadership of Rewi Maniapoto, held out for three days. Because they were surrounded, were without water and short of ammunition, they were invited to surrender. The story goes that Rewi Maniapoto replied: 'Ka whawhai tonu ake! Ake! Ake! (We will fight on forever, forever, forever!)' They were asked to send out the women and children and Ahumai Te Paerata rose up and declaimed that the women would sooner die with the men than live without them.

The Maori made a daring daylight escape in good order. Fewer than half of them made it but Rewi did. Many, including women and children, were cut down by pursuing infantry and a detachment of cavalry. It was a comprehensive military defeat. And by defending the land they lived on, so many of them to the death, Maori ensured they would lose it through confiscation. After the battle, the land was allocated as a farm to William Cowan. Cowan's son, James, a famous journalist and historian, was raised there, a life he described in *The Old Frontier*, one of his many books.

Maori failed at Orakau for two reasons: first, a brilliant outflanking movement by British regulars, undetected by Maori, took them to the heart of the Kingite homeland; and secondly, the pa at Orakau had, uncharacteristically, been built with no escape route. Rewi had been aware of the

Rewi Maniapoto lost the Battle of Orakau in March 1864, but won perhaps the greatest public relations campaign in New Zealand history by writing his name in legend with his vow to fight on forever and ever when invited to surrender. The women, invited to leave the Orakau pa, insisted on staying with their men. About half the three hundred Maori in the pa escaped after an orderly daylight retreat.

The Rewi legend was embellished in the 1920s when pioneer film-maker Rudall Hayward released his silent movie, Rewi's Last Stand. Hayward made another version with sound fifteen years later and it was released at the time of the 1940 centennial celebrations. Hayward, in association with A. W. Reed, also issued a novel illustrated with stills from the film.

inadequacy of the site and hadn't at first wanted to make a stand there, but was persuaded to.

So, after a series of brilliantly conducted battles against the odds in Taranaki and Waikato, this defeat – mythologised as Rewi's Last Stand – grasped the imagination of New Zealanders and holds it to this day. The Maori's disciplined but defiant courage also earned the admiration of British professional soldiers and military historians. Among other results, it inspired New Zealand's first full-length film, Rudall Hayward's *Rewi's Last Stand*.

Later that month, a force under General Cameron attacked Ngai Te Rangi led by Rawiri Tuaia at Gate Pa, near Tauranga, and suffered a defeat so comprehensive it threw the civil and military into a panic of incomprehension. About 250 Maori sat out the heaviest artillery barrage used by the British during the New Zealand Wars, so severe it was a microcosm of the barrage that launched the Battle of the Somme fifty years later. The defences were breached, an assault seemed successful, when suddenly the defenders opened fire from hidden bunkers and caused a rout, sending experienced soldiers and marines fleeing in panic, leaving more than a hundred dead and wounded behind. Maori, who claimed only twenty-five dead, escaped during the night.

🪶 🪶 🪶

Pakeha then had successes as the Waikato War lingered on towards its inevitable end. The regulars left the country in the late 1860s and the colonists, backed by Maori 'friendlies', as they were called, fought through a long series of skirmishes in Taranaki and the East Coast with mixed results. Maori sects loosely based on the Old Testament, such as the Hauhau (Pai Marire) and Ringatu, sprang up and inspired attacks on settlers. Two formidable leaders, Te Kooti on the East Coast, and Titokowaru in Taranaki, provided the last serious blaze of Maori resistance.

Te Kooti was in his mid-thirties when he was sent to the Chatham Islands as a prisoner in 1866. He became the leader of about 160 exiled Maori prisoners on the island and organised a well-planned and efficiently executed escape, raiding the islands' armoury and taking over a schooner, the *Rifleman*. They treated the guards they overpowered well and when they landed in Poverty Bay told government representatives they were moving inland and had no intention of fighting unless pursued and attacked. Te Kooti was now a religious as well as a political leader, a prophet of 'Ringatu', the Upraised Hand, after studying the Old Testament while in the Chathams.

He was pursued by a force including the Armed Constabulary, local militia and friendly Maori, led by a British officer, Colonel Whitmore. A skilled guerrilla fighter, Te Kooti kept large numbers of opponents busy. He was elusive, capable of moving swiftly through the bush despite a large accompanying troop of non-combatants, and when the enemy came close he fought with courage and panache. After three years, he escaped in 1872 to the King Country. Te Kooti was at first seen as a kind of bogeyman by settlers but became a mythic figure, the hero of many tales and captured in fiction by Maurice Shadbolt.

But the name Titokowaru disappeared from history for more than a century, lying inert in newspapers and archives until resurrected in the 1980s by historian James Belich. No military historians had for a long time, if ever, seriously examined the details of the civil war with Maori until Christopher Pugsley investigated the pa, especially Ruapekapeka. Belich, a professional historian, looked closely at each of the battles fought, analysing tactics and outcomes. His revisionist history emerged in a powerful book, *The New Zealand Wars and the Victorian Interpretation of Racial Conflict*, in 1986, and he later presented a television series on the wars. Titokowaru emerged in this book as one of the most

Te Kooti escaped from exile in the Chatham Islands by commandeering a ship and landing in Poverty Bay. He became a formidable guerrilla leader from the East Coast of the North Island. During his exile he had studied the Old Testament and developed his own religion called 'Ringatu', the 'Upraised Hand'. After a three-year campaign he escaped to the King Country in 1872 and was left alone.

Major von Tempsky from Germany distinguished himself as a brilliant guerrilla leader with his Forest Rangers who took part in a number of campaigns during the New Zealand Wars. He was killed in action during the uprising under Titokowaru in Taranaki. Titokowaru's rebellion was little known until historian James Belich wrote his The New Zealand Wars, *published in 1986, followed by* I Shall Not Die: Titokowaru's War *three years later. The rebellion was initially successful but faded away when the astute Maori commander lost mana and was deserted by his men.*
(Alexander Turnbull Library, Making New Zealand Collection, MNZ876)

intelligent, cool and brave Maori generals. Later that decade, Belich wrote *I Shall Not Die, Titokowaru's War* and at last told the full story of the short but scarily effective campaign in South Taranaki in 1868–69.

Titokowaru was an advocate for peace after the major Taranaki campaign early in the 1860s, but was roused to fight when settlers began to move onto the land occupied by his Ngaruahine people. After raids in which settlers were killed, he was pursued to his village deep in the bush by colonial troops, including the Armed Constabulary, and the Forest Rangers led by Von Tempsky, who was killed in action during this campaign.

The first attempt to root the rebellious chief from his base ended in a disastrous defeat for the colonial army. Thus Titokowaru gained control over most of the land between Mt Taranaki and Wanganui but failed to quickly drive his advantage home. Next, he lured the troops to a pa he had established at Moturoa. Again, he out-thought and outfought the colonials, according to Belich, and panicked both the provincial and central authorities.

The threat came to an end when Titokowaru's followers left him, virtually overnight – apparently because of a mysterious loss of mana – as he prepared to resist yet another assault. The pa they had built was abandoned. Although he remained at large with a small force he ceased to be a threat, and the likelihood was gone that further success would have ignited a large-scale uprising by Maori in Taranaki and Waikato. One explanation for his men drifting away was that he had a sexual liaison with the wife of one of his fellow warriors. But no certain explanation is known.

By 1872, the serious conflict between the races was over but for a Christian-style, passive-resistance campaign at Parihaka, in northern Taranaki, by Te Whiti-o-Rongomai, during which he and his community were harassed by government forces and then he and his associate, Tohu Kakahi, were arrested and held for two years without trial. They were later allowed to return to Parihaka.

Maori were left with a bitter sense of betrayal, and with a

Te Whiti-o-Rongomai launched a passive resistance campaign at Parihaka in Taranaki in 1872 over what his people considered was their land. He and his community were harassed by government forces and he and his associate Tohu Kakahi were arrested and held for two years without trial. They were later allowed to return to Parihaka. Their story won wide attention a hundred years on with the publication of author Dick Scott's book, Ask That Mountain. (Alexander Turnbull Library, G.M. Preston Collection, PAI-0-423-10-4)

feeling they were marginalised. At the same time, the realisation surfaced among Pakeha that Maori had been tough, talented and chivalrous opponents who had been enormously respected by the professional British soldiers. Because settlers were safe at last to expand unchallenged, the mood changed to one of romantic condescension, tinged perhaps with guilt.

Chapter Eight:

DEFEAT AND REVIVAL

I N DEFEAT, MAORI faced severe retribution. The confiscation of more than 1.2 million hectares of their land in Taranaki, Waikato, Bay of Plenty, the East Coast and elsewhere after the war was called by historian Keith Sinclair: '. . . the worst injustice ever perpetrated by a New Zealand Government.' The confiscation was punitive only in concept because the best land was taken, not necessarily that which belonged to those who had 'rebelled'.

Among many Pakeha this misappropriation was justified by a popular, conscience-salving, piece of casuistry: by accepting British 'sovereignty' under the Treaty of Waitangi, Maori became subject to British law, and therefore they should accept decisions on land ownership by the government (in which they had no part, despite citizenship); and, anyway, Maori should acquiesce because taking land by conquest and occupying it was justified by their own former law. They were damned by selected parts of both laws.

Equally self-serving was the claim that settlers needed the land to make it fully productive, that Maori were not 'using' it – that is, farming it pastorally – and therefore lost the right to hold it. Thus Pakeha could have it both ways. Even as late as the 1970s, a Pakeha said to me that 'unproductive' Maori land should be given to farmers who would 'work it'. I asked him how that sat with the British reverence for private property, and how he felt about confiscating land from their aristocracy – even the royal family – if it was landscaped only for their own aesthetic satisfaction around their castles, or kept in trees and lakes solely for seasonal hunting expeditions. He said that was 'different'.

For New Zealanders of my and my father's generations with an abiding interest in our history, the last forty years of the twentieth century were a journey of enlightenment. From 1890 until the 1960s, the story of the settlement of New Zealand and the context of race relations was written mostly in the tone of the boys' adventure magazines we grew up with. This left us with an immature and fantastical idea of our origin as a nation, encased as it was in the assumption that the British were invincible and the major civilising force for good in the world. We lived in the nirvana of this illusion. After describing the British and colonial forces as 'our men' and 'our boys', A. H. Reed in *The Story of New Zealand* ended his account of the Taranaki War thus:

> . . . the settlers, with brave hearts, set to work to rebuild their homes. Once more the Taranaki hills and valleys were dotted with cattle and sheep. Once more grain was grown, and harvests reaped, and fruit gathered from the orchards. Once more the settlers and their wives and children walked at close of day in their gardens, gay with the flowers of old Devon.

Of the fate of Maori, not a word.

During the Waikato War, Maori were nursing 'grievances or supposed grievances', he wrote. Those who would not affirm their loyalty and obedience to the Queen, hid themselves in the bush and 'caused a great deal of trouble'. His account of Te Whiti's passive-resistance campaign is like a children's Christmas story:

> The Maori came off victorious in the strange kind of warfare. They were generously given full possession of the land and Te Whiti returned to Parihaka in triumph.

Sir Peter Buck (Te Rangi Hiroa) was an athlete, physician, administrator, politician, soldier and anthropologist who became internationally known as an expert on Polynesia and the Polynesians. Educated at Te Aute College in Hawke's Bay and at Otago University College, he was a member of a generation of young Maori who were influential politically, and became outstanding role models for their peers and successors. Buck rose to second in command of the NZ Pioneer Battalion in World War I. He became Professor of Anthropology at Yale University in the US and then Director (later President of the Board of Trustees) of the Bishop Museum in Hawaii.
(Alexander Turnbull Library, S.P. Andrew Collection, F-19099-1/1, photographer S.P. Andrew, 1935)

Many New Zealanders raised on this sort of history were therefore hurt when historians, starting with Sinclair, began delivering professional, revised versions. He has been followed by authors such as Michael King, James Belich, Anne Salmond and Claudia Orange who disinterred primary sources, and looked behind the contemporary accounts of the post-European Maori story as it was told by representatives of the victorious, dominant culture.

As historians have stripped back layers of well-meant sentimentality and myth from the story of New Zealand in the nineteenth century, we can look at it in a more realistic and nation-affirming way. Maori undoubtedly thought the Treaty of Waitangi left them some sovereignty, some right to govern themselves, or at least some significant say in how they would be governed. When the settlers arrived they found a temperate-zone country they could convert to something like the agricultural and pastoral landscape of 'home', or 'the old country', except that they would own the land and not be victims of landlordism. By shaping what they saw as this raw country into a better, more productive economy than they had left behind, they would build a prosperous future and do everyone a great favour. To them, Maori were brave children and the Treaty of Waitangi an acknowledgement of British sovereignty.

🌿 🌿 🌿

After 1865, Kingites retreated into 1100 square kilometres of what is now known as the King Country, most of it rugged country settlers didn't want. Europeans were warned that if they crossed the border they would be killed – and some were. But the search for a share of power never went away. Kotahitanga, a Maori Parliament was set up in 1892, and the first revival of Maori influence arose with a Young Maori Party designed to improve health and morale. It included Apirana Ngata, Peter Buck (Te Rangi Hiroa), Maui Pomare, Frederick Bennett and other outstanding, educated young men.

Maori and their land weren't parted only by war. Legislation and courts made it easier and easier for them to sell despite the tangle of who held title. As late as the 1960s, legislation made Maori land accessible to general buyers where it was 'in the public interest' in the opinion of 'improvement inspectors'.

By the end of the nineteenth century, Maori had seemed beaten and bowed. Some observers predicted their eventual demise as a race. But in fact the tide was turning. The Maori population in 1898 was around 42,000, down sixty per cent in sixty years. Ten years later it was approaching 48,000 and the birth rate was rising. The prevailing wisdom at the time among both Maori and Pakeha was that assimilation was the answer for the future. Maoritanga was suppressed in the education system in a bid to Europeanise youngsters to take part in modern New Zealand society. Maori had been given four seats in Parliament as early as 1867 but their successful MPs, including members of the Young Maori Party, tended to favour assimilation. For example, a vigorous worker for his people, Maui Pomare, was nevertheless the weight behind the Tohunga Suppression Act of 1907.

Maori and Pakeha had from the beginning found each other attractive people and the rate of intermarriage was always high compared with most countries in which Europeans had settled in the great age of colonial expansion – and in this sense 'assimilation' continues today.

Sir Maui Pomare was another influential young Maori who became a physician. He was elected to Parliament for Western Maori in 1911, and was a Minister without portfolio in William Massey's first administration. He was Minister of Health and of Internal Affairs during his nineteen years in the House.
(Alexander Turnbull Library, S.P. Andrew Collection, G-14583-1/1, photographer S.P. Andrew, 1912)

During the war, the settlers would grant that Maori were daring and resourceful for 'natives', but considered the European fighting man inherently superior, smarter and better disciplined. To sustain this view they papered over the fact of their obvious defeats by blaming ill luck, or incompetence of commanders, and even turned defeats into victories by exaggerating Maori casualties. The record now shows that Maori were almost invariably outnumbered and outgunned; that they were on important occasions superbly controlled

This famous NZ Herald picture depicts the revered leader Dame Whina Cooper leading a 'not one acre more' land march from Te Hapua in Northland to Parliament in Wellington in 1975. She personified a new attitude of Maori assertiveness.

and disciplined; and that to counter their disadvantages they devised strategically shrewd and innovative plans, backed by surprising engineering skills.

The British forces had superior resources and a logistical infrastructure Maori could never match. And yet at Ohaeawai in Northland, at Puketakauere in Taranaki, at Gate Pa in the Bay of Plenty and during the campaign against Titokowaru, the British suffered defeats at the hands of smaller armies that shocked them; and at Orakau, they were humbled by the discipline and valour of those they overwhelmed. And none of that detracts from the ability of the British regulars who had shown in many countries they were dogged, courageous and capable. The settler forces too proved resourceful and brave.

The Maori achievement was extraordinary, though, and perhaps even more remarkable was their comeback in the 1970s, which led to the setting up of the Waitangi Tribunal to investigate grievances associated with the Treaty. A series of events demonstrated a new, assertive attitude. In 1975, the revered Whina Cooper led a 'not one acre more' land march from Te Hapua in Northland to Parliament. Ngati Whatua defied the government for five years to hold its land at Bastion Point in Auckland. Maori studies programmes sprang up at universities. A cultural awakening was under way as Maori population expanded and young leaders gained confidence. At the same time, the continuing controversy over New Zealand rugby teams playing in South Africa under apartheid raised awareness of the destructive consequences of racism. By the end of the twentieth century, Maori had become a potent force in New Zealand politics, claiming expanding rights under the Treaty of Waitangi, which had become a more influential document than at any previous time in 160 years of existence.

Perhaps the most important work of the Waitangi Tribunal has been to reconcile past differences, to heal over the past. In many parts of the world old wounds keep suppurating centuries after crimes against people were committed and after crimes were then committed in retaliation. In Northern Ireland, for example, they are still fighting the Battle of the Boyne six hundred years after the last shot was fired. So redress and reconciliation for Maori have been important for the future of New Zealand.

Maori were, however, historically lucky. First, the European intrusion into the South Pacific was led by James Cook,

79

Ngati Whatua defied the government for five years in an unyielding and ultimately successful fight to retain its land at Auckland's Bastion Point.

unusually for his time a patient humanitarian, enlightened in his attitude towards indigenous people. A European arrival in the eighteenth century was inevitable. The French explorer de Surville was here within two months of Cook's first visit, and the early French contacts with Maori were disastrous. Clashes between the disparate European and Maori cultures were unavoidable and, because of the technological superiority of guns, Maori were bound to suffer in these early exchanges. But Cook, often at great personal risk, consistently avoided applying unnecessary force to the point of alienating his own men.

Then, when the British government decided, with some reluctance, to make New Zealand a colony, it did so with regard for the rights of Maori through the Treaty, a consideration never seriously offered to the millions of indigenous people in the Americas, Africa or Australia. Timing helped. The Great Emancipation Act was passed in the British Parliament in 1833, providing for gradual freeing of slaves throughout its colonies. As the Treaty was being signed, house slaves on the West Indian colonial plantations had been set free and field slaves gained their liberty a year later. At the time the Great Emancipation Act was passed, *The Times* editorialised in London on:

The increasing voice of enlightened humanity – a growing respect
for the rights of human nature – the diffusion of information on
the barbarities of the colonial system – the new power of the
pulpit, the hustings, and the press in spreading knowledge on the
state of the colonies . . . must have convinced any Ministry that
the abominations of the slave system could not be tolerated
much longer.

This growing British sense of shame at colonial abuse
undoubtedly worked as much in favour of Maori survival as
their own dogged physical and moral courage. Indeed, as their
own behaviour during the Musket Wars of the 1830s and
during their ruthless killing of Moriori after invading the
Chatham Islands demonstrated, their own impulses towards
the colonised had needed to change sharply too.

Also, to see the land question clearly, it is not fair to assume
that only Maori had a special spiritual attachment to it
whereas the Pakeha attitude was nakedly commercial and
utilitarian. Squatters with capital did run sheep over large
areas of the South Island simply to make money from wool,
the way fortunes were being made in Australia, and many
returned to Britain after multiplying their investment. In
Canterbury particularly, huge areas were under the control
of a handful of runholders until the 1880s and 1890s, from
when the properties were gradually broken up.

But from the 1870s thousands of families were cutting into
the North Island forest to create small farms for themselves.
Much of the Forty-Mile Bush that ran north from the top of
Wairarapa into Hawke's Bay was felled by Scandinavian
immigrants. The dense rainforest in Taranaki was attacked
early and for many years the flat areas of the province looked
like a moonscape as smallholders and their families worked
on a pastoral frontier, cutting and burning the trees and
sowing grass around the stumps to carry dairy cattle and sheep.
They were encouraged by government legislation designed
to open up Crown land, and they were enthused by the
growth of the dairy industry which tacked an income onto
subsistence farming. These immigrants, certainly more than

one-third of the total, were not capitalist runholders but poorly paid former British labourers, farm workers or tenant farmers; or from the lower middleclass; or, in the case of the Scots and Irish, refugees from what they had once regarded as their own land. They were unequivocally aware of the security and status land provided.

Romantic notions of pre-industrial, bucolic bliss among Britons in what had not long before been a purely agricultural economy imbued them with an attachment to land that was in many ways also spiritual. They understood what Thomas Carlyle had so forcefully written:

> It is well said, 'Land is the right basis of an Aristocracy'; whoever possesses the land, he, more emphatically than any other, is the Governor, Viceking of the people on the land. It is these days [1843] as it was in those of Henry Plantagenet and Abbot Samson; as it will in all days be. The land is Mother of us all; nourishes, shelters, gladdens, lovingly enriches us all . . .

Many New Zealand immigrants saw themselves as a new egalitarian aristocracy, and land ownership was critical to that vision. This was reflected later in the quarter-acre section pride of the towns and cities. The home garden with its range of vegetables and flowers became an integral part of any definition of New Zealanders' culture.

All these factors worked towards an evolving New Zealand national attitude of tolerance and open-mindedness. Maori have done better than any other of the indigenous peoples dominated by European colonial powers since the eighteenth century, not only because of their own indomitable attitude but also because Pakeha New Zealanders, since World War II especially, have tried earnestly, if often enough irritably, to reconcile historical differences in search of that fabulous destination – a fair go for all.

Chapter Nine:

PAKEHA SETTLEMENT

THE FIRST NEW ZEALAND Company was set up in London in the early 1820s and failed at an attempt to colonise; so was later largely ignored by historians. Among its wealthy and influential principals was John Lambton (later Lord Durham), who was a link to the second New Zealand Company. The first company raised £20,000 to promote settlement. A preliminary expedition of two ships, the *Rosanna* and the *Lambton*, arrived at Stewart Island early in 1826 with about sixty artisans and mechanics aboard. The ships proceeded to Dunedin Harbour, Port Nicholson, the Hauraki Gulf (where they bought Waiheke Island from Maori) and on to land the company bought in the Hokianga.

Historian A. H. McLintock said members of the expedition were 'uneasy at the thought of meeting the ferocious savages of the north' and found the reception 'so unpromising' when they arrived that they moved on to Sydney. But Peter B. Maling notes in his *Historic Charts and Maps of New Zealand* that the leader of the expedition, Captain James Herd, had visited New Zealand previously and Maori had told Samuel Marsden they would kill him if he stayed because he had been so unscrupulous a trader. After the project failed, the company dissolved. Herd deserves a place in history, though, because he was the first to chart both Otago Harbour and Port Nicholson (both missed by Cook).

In 1837, the New Zealand Association was formed in London

A portrait of Edward Gibbon Wakefield looms over his great-granddaughters, Misses Irma and Beryl O'Connor, at a morning tea in Wakefield House, Wellington, given in honour of the memory of the man whose philosophy of migration and colonial settlement had a profound effect on the history of New Zealand. Wakefield was a recklessly romantic youth. The second of his two runaway marriages ended in a prison term and disqualified him from what would probably have been a distinguished political career in Britain. He was involved in Canadian colonial settlement and in the establishment of South Australia, and his association with the New Zealand Company led to the kitset settlements in Wellington, Nelson, New Plymouth, Wanganui, Christchurch and Dunedin. His brothers, William, Arthur, Felix and David, his son Edward Jerningham, and nephews Oliver and Edward all lived in New Zealand for a time. Edward Gibbon sailed for New Zealand from London in 1852 and became a member of the Wellington Provincial Council and the House of Representatives. The story of the family is told by Philip Temple in A Sort of Conscience.

to recruit English emigrants for New Zealand according to a plan conceived by Edward Gibbon Wakefield. It became a joint stock company in 1839 with a capital of £100,000 and a number of influential men among its directors, including Lord Durham. Wakefield was a powerful presence within the company, but unofficially because a three-year jail term for the abduction of a girl had driven his influence into back rooms.

The trouble was New Zealand was still an independent country under the control of Maori, despite the presence of many Europeans, including missionaries. A vacillating British government couldn't make up its mind on a policy. Investors and restless would-be emigrants wanted a colony, while the Church Missionary Society wanted some sort of government protection for Maori and not a flood of immigrants. Worried the government would make any formal settlement difficult, or even proscribe it, the company hurriedly went ahead with its colonisation plans.

The first party of settlers sponsored by this New Zealand Company sailed into Wellington aboard the Aurora two weeks before the signing of the Treaty of Waitangi and, thus, before annexation was a deal. An advance party led by Edward Gibbon's brother, Colonel William Wakefield, with Edward Jerningham, his son, had arrived the previous August aboard the company-owned Tory to reconnoitre, report back and buy land – even though the decision to send settlers had been made. The company's programme added to pressure on the British government to subsume New Zealand within the empire by implying that settlement could not be stopped.

At the time, Britain was suffering widespread unemployment. A large stratum of restless poor threatened peace and good order; so it wasn't hard to find people to flee the factory

84

towns. Edward Gibbon Wakefield's plan was to avoid convict colonies and the haphazard type of settlement of the United States and Canada by exporting compact agricultural communities based on the social classes of England. Revenue from land sold to members of colonising communities would provide for continuing emigration. Britain would thus be a better country, and a flourishing little Albion would be established in the South Pacific.

Wakefield's ideas were bold and coherent and had a powerful effect on New Zealand's development. But it would have been amazing if everything had gone according to plan, given the disorganised nature of New Zealand at the time. When the early parties arrived to settle in Wellington, Nelson, New Plymouth and Wanganui, Hobson was still trying to set up some sort of realistic administration. To the newcomers, New Zealand was a kind of brochure-land. Few had any real knowledge of the place except for what they had read or been told, usually third-hand. To add to the confusion, once the Treaty was signed, land titles were reviewed. How much land the company actually owned, and where, was vague and often disputed.

The company immigrants regarded themselves as the only serious settlers of the new country and conducted their affairs as though the colonial government was irrelevant. The Wellingtonians were contemptuous of the early governors and annoyed that they didn't move the capital to their new town. But during the early 1840s, these Wellington settlers went through a crisis of disenchantment, which they blamed

The Tory *and the* Cuba *meet in Cook Strait in 1840, envisioned by Charles Heaphy. The ships were chartered by the New Zealand Company to bring land purchasers and surveyors to Wellington in 1839, in preparation for the first party of settlers who arrived in the* Aurora *in 1840.*

on the British government, the governors and Maori, as well as the management of the company. The woes were the result of unfulfilled company contracts, wildly inaccurate surveys, registers and titles, and tension with Maori on land ownership.

The *Aurora* group disembarked at 'Britannia', on the Hutt Valley side of Port Nicholson, in 1840. When the Hutt River flooded, they moved to the site Wellington city occupies today. It was hardly an auspicious start and pioneers must have had reservations about their new home when an earthquake in 1848 toppled brick structures. Seven years later, what experts guess was probably the country's biggest earthquake of modern times changed the contours of the surrounding landscape.

The availability of land in Wellington was an issue from the start of settlement. There was not much of it and local Maori were intractable, although without them the new-comers would have quickly starved. So Wanganui was settled the following year as an offshoot of the Wellington community and some farmers with the money to buy sheep moved into the Wairarapa.

The *William Bryan* arrived at New Plymouth in March 1841 with New Zealand Company settlers from Devon and Cornwall. In 1842, the *Fifeshire*, *Mary Ann*, *Lloyds* and *Lord Auckland* arrived in Nelson with around 3000 new settlers from in or around London. Captain Arthur Wakefield, another of the brothers, had been sent ahead to manage this new community and buy land; and confusion over who owned what land led to his death in the Wairau Affray in 1843.

Edward Wakefield's ideas inspired settlement in 1848 by the Otago Association, which was controlled by a schismatic Presbyterian Church group called the Free Church of Scotland. He was even more deeply involved in the establishment of Canterbury in 1850 by the Canterbury Association, dominated by the Anglican Church. Invercargill was established by government allocation of land in 1857, and Timaru two years later.

Other substantial, organised migrations, but not

Wakefieldian, included: English Nonconformists to Albertland, on the Kaipara Harbour in Northland, in the early 1860s; Scottish Highlanders to Waipu in the 1850s; Czechoslovakians to Puhoi, Scandinavians to southern Hawke's Bay and Manawatu, and Mancunians to Manawatu from the 1860s; and Ulstermen to Katikati and Poles to Taranaki in the 1870s.

So although Wakefield's compact, carefully stratified communities didn't develop according to plan, many New Zealand towns and cities did begin with common interest groups whose members looked forward to an affluent life in a new land.

The settlements were scattered around the coastline and communications were poor; so poor in the case of Albertland that most people soon left their allocated land and moved to Auckland. But by and large these were independent and strong-minded people or they wouldn't have made the journey, and they made the best of their new circumstances.

Hobson set up his capital in Auckland with its accessibility to Port Jackson, Sydney, from where most of the early New Zealand administrators came. He was a sickly man and, after he died in office in 1842, was succeeded by Colonial Secretary Willoughby Shortland as Administrator. Shortland filled in for more than a year until the next Governor, Captain Robert FitzRoy arrived. FitzRoy had been commander of the *Beagle* when it carried Charles Darwin around the world, the journey during which the theory of evolution took shape in the great biologist's mind. Hobson, Shortland and FitzRoy governed in a muddled, autocratic way on the end of a string from London. In the years after annexation, the colony was in a financial mess because neither Britain nor the New South Wales administration wanted to put up any money.

The settlers, particularly those in the south, despised the governors' tendency to intercede between their ambitions and what Britain perceived as the needs of Maori, and they vociferously sought more say in the conduct of their own

Captain Robert FitzRoy was Governor for two years from December 1843 but became intensely disliked, especially in Wellington and Nelson, partly because of his haughty manner but mostly because he ruled that the settlers and not Maori had been the prime cause of the Wairau Affray. FitzRoy was captain of the HMS Beagle during its famous journey around the world with naturalist Charles Darwin aboard. When he arrived to take office, the colony was in a state of unrest. He was recalled by the Colonial Office before his term was up.
(Alexander Turnbull Library, Schmidt Collection, G13181/1)

Commander Willoughby Shortland served in the Royal Navy with William Hobson, came to New Zealand as Police Magistrate in 1840, served under Hobson as the Colonial Secretary and took over as Administrator in 1842 when Hobson died. He held office until Hobson's successor as Governor, Robert FitzRoy, arrived fifteen months later. Shortland was sacked by FitzRoy as Colonial Secretary soon after his arrival. A younger brother, Dr Edward Shortland, who had been private secretary to Hobson, later practised medicine in Auckland and became an authority on Maori language and lore.

affairs. The Cook Strait New Zealand Company settlements especially resented the capital being in Auckland. They wanted to govern themselves. They reserved a special dislike for the overbearing FitzRoy, who seemed to want to run the colony as he would a Royal Navy ship. The newspapers called him an imbecile and persistently questioned his fitness for office. When he was recalled before his term was up, Wellingtonians celebrated by carrying his effigies through the town and burning them.

All this time, Maori were increasingly apprehensive about the number of arrivals and the government's disregard of their rights and interests.

So it was hardly an auspicious start for the brave new little world of New Zealand.

And then, in 1845, Captain George Edward Grey arrived with all the hustle and confidence of a hungrily ambitious 33-year-old, fresh from a successful term as Governor of South Australia, the one Australian settlement that owed its origins to Wakefield's colonising philosophy. Sandhurst-educated, he had served in Ireland where he must have seen what disruption land tenure problems could cause. He was clever and imaginative, enjoyed the exercise of power, and had no intention of letting settlers erode his influence; so he stalled any extension of popular government as long as he could. Grey never did get the hang of democracy, as his later parliamentary career demonstrated.

The British government, though, wanted some self-government as soon as it decently could, and settlers were nagging for it. The country was divided into New Munster (north from the middle of the North Island) and New Ulster (south from there). Plans were made for an intricate pyramid of government from local councils to provincial assemblies to a national assembly, topped by the governor. The proposal stalled and Grey just got on with his policies, which had to attend to serious financial and administration problems. He made a genuine attempt to tame Maori and make them fit into a Europeanised society.

Grey is a central figure in New Zealand's early history

George Edward Grey was a central figure in nineteenth-century New Zealand history with two terms as Governor (1845–53, 1861–68) and one as Prime Minister (1877–79). Grey's decisive nature made him a better Governor than a Prime Minister, but his Liberal Party was an early attempt to build a government around a party philosophy. Grey was born in Lisbon a few days after the death of his father during the Battle of Badajoz in Spain. He was educated at Sandhurst and served in Ireland where land tenure problems turned him into a political liberal. He spent three years exploring in Australia before his appointment in 1840 as Governor of the Wakefield-style settlement in South Australia. Between his first and second terms in New Zealand he was Governor of Cape Colony and High Commissioner for South Africa. He went to London after his second term as Governor here and tried unsuccessfully to enter the House of Commons. On his return, he became Superintendent of Auckland Province and then was an MP for twenty years. Grey, who developed an abiding interest in Maori legends and folklore, died while in London and was buried in St Paul's Cathedral.

because he was shrewd and decisive during his first term of office and attempted to fully understand Maori, a style that contrasted sharply with the three men who had preceded him and the two who followed. He was manipulative and self-serving in his reports to the British government, which helped him have his way fairly consistently and made him at least an effective, on-the-spot administrator. His first term ended in 1853, a few months after the first electoral government was put in place. His second term was from 1861 to 1868.

A form of self-government was established by the New Zealand Constitution Act passed by the British Parliament in 1852. It provided for provincial government in six provinces: Auckland, New Plymouth, Wellington, Nelson, Canterbury and Otago. This happened against a background of continuing, often rabid internecine squabbling as provincial councils tried to arrogate as much power as they could from the Governor and a General Assembly, and as they fought among themselves on parochial issues. Before long new provinces began breaking away from the original six: Hawke's Bay from Wellington (1858), Marlborough from Nelson (1859), and Southland from Otago (1861, but rejoined in 1870). Remote and rugged Westland was at first lumped in with Canterbury but became a separate province in 1868 as its population burgeoned following the discovery of gold. New Plymouth became Taranaki in 1859.

The superior power in this new government structure, above the provincial councils, resided in a General Assembly, set up at the same time, and a Legislative Council, whose members were appointed for life; a term cut to seven years in the 1890s. Maori policy remained with the Governor and foreign policy with Britain. But most settlers were more interested in their provincial councils than the parliament in Auckland which first met in May 1854 but didn't start serious law-making until two years later.

Executive power at national level was shuffled around the same men in a series of early administrations, as though General Assembly members were dancing quadrilles. Because only those of independent means could afford the time to invest in politics, a relatively small group of well-off, educated men from the Wakefield-style towns changed partners regularly to form new ministries often based on parochial issues and personal likes and antipathies. But the dancers remained pretty well the same – what Keith Sinclair called 'an oligarchy chiefly representative of pastoralists and speculators'.

Between 1856 and 1893, nine ministries lasted more than eighteen months, only four of these lasted three years and only one of them for five years. During that period, Edward Stafford was Premier three times for a total of nearly nine years and yet was a peculiarly undistinguished figure who left no substantial imprint on history. He held office longer than William Fox and Harry Atkinson combined, even though they were each Premier four times. Stafford's virtue seemed to be an ability to mollify opposing forces, stand above personalities and walk between the interests of the provincial and national assemblies. A small man, and especially hirsute even for those times, he was an excellent jockey, loved the life of the gentry and didn't really find New Zealand congenial. He fled back to Britain once out of office. But, with the much more astute Vogel, he did help to dissolve provincial government in 1876, thus concentrating power in the national government.

All in all, they weren't venal men but were self-serving in a class and business sense. They were also quarrelsome and vituperative. It wasn't until the Long Depression of the 1880s that sharp philosophical differences finally rose above single issues and personalities and drove politicians into radical and conservative party camps.

But beneath all the political blather, what was really going on at the grassroots in the colony? And grass roots is the *mot juste* because from very early the economic foundations of the colony rested on pasture. It was no secret that there was money in wool. Fortunes had been made in Australia by squatters who ran sheep over that country's seemingly limitless stretches of sparse grassland. Canterbury similarly had tussock plains, except on a smaller scale, and among the first arrivals after the Canterbury Association settlers were a number of Australian sheepmen, or 'Shagroons', as they were called. They and their sheep were refugees from a severe drought across the Tasman.

But wool-growing on any scale started in the Wairarapa as early as 1843 when Charles Bidwell and William Swainson drove about 350, mostly in-lamb merino ewes around the south coastal route from Wellington into the Wairarapa valley. With autumn closing in on winter, they had to carry the

Frederick Weld was a member of a prominent English Catholic family and was among the founders of sheep-farming in New Zealand. A few days after he arrived in 1844, he joined Charles Clifford, William Vavasour and Henry Petre to drove 600 sheep from Wellington into the Wairarapa, across the rocks at Mukamuka, on the bleak southern coast of the North Island. Weld later moved to the more expansive and drier Wairau Plain in Marlborough, and in 1851 wrote Hints to Intending Sheep Farmers in NZ. *He became the MP for Wairau in 1853 and later represented Cheviot, and was Premier for a year from 1864. He was influential in having the capital transferred from Auckland to Wellington. After he returned to England, Weld became a top British colonial administrator as Governor of Western Australia, of Tasmania and the Straits Settlements.*

animals, one by one, across the Mukamuka rocks: 'A work of time,' said Bidwell, 'but which was accompanied with less trouble than we expected and without any loss.'

Four others, all members of a prominent, extended English Catholic family – Frederick Weld (later Premier of the colony), Charles Clifford, William Vavasour and Henry Petre – took the same route at the same time with 600 sheep. They were passed by Bidwell and Swainson as they drove their larger flock around the wind-thrashed southern beaches, and they lost some animals during the manhandling at Mukamuka as the weather got worse. This group had leased a square mile of grass and scrubland from local Maori for £12 a year. Only about 800 Ngati Kahungunu were living in the Wairarapa at the time.

These colonists with capital were responding to reports from the few people who had already looked into the Wairarapa because so little satisfactory pasture land was available close to the new Wellington settlement. A New Zealand Company surveyor, Charles Brees, had walked over the hills from the Hutt Valley the previous year and reported an abundance of prairie grass and fernland for pastoral purposes, enough timber for building and fuel, and 'quite sufficient land for arable purposes to suit settlers'. Within two years of Bidwell and Swainson's arrival, twelve sheep stations were established in the area.

However, the merinos suffered severe foot problems on the damp floor of the valley and it was only after some experienced Scottish shepherds moved the flocks onto the slopes that they began to flourish. But for this and other reasons, squatters favoured the dry tussock plains and hill country of Canterbury, Hawke's Bay, Marlborough and Otago for running their merinos as the industry developed over the next few decades. Some of the original Wairarapa settlers sold up and joined them. Go south young man became the call. Men with capital realised that the South Island – relatively free from land hassles with Maori and much of it already clear of bush – was the place to run sheep and make money.

It's not too much to say the South Island became another country as Maori fiercely contested land ownership and political power north of Cook Strait. For example, Englishman Robert B. Booth wrote a book called *Five Years in New Zealand (1859 to 1864)* without ever mentioning the war in Taranaki and Waikato, recounting only his life among the sheep and on the goldfields of the south. In fact, he mentioned Maori only in his general introduction.

Wellington was an unhappy community in its earliest years, its settlers languishing from want of land and opportunity, although it gained much from becoming the nation's capital in 1865. Meanwhile, unplanned Auckland continued to grow briskly from its origins as a government centre and garrison town. Its economy was based on timber, kauri gum and agriculture, and later on a financial industry. Settlers were pushing back from the small commercial centre on the edge of the Waitemata Harbour, past Epsom and other latter-day inner suburbs, towards Mangere and the rich soils of South Auckland. Cows were milked, crops grown and steers slaughtered to feed the locals and to supply the ships that came from around the Pacific. The settlement was scornfully referred to as Little Sydney by some southerners and it was true that about half its immigrants came from New South Wales.

This wasn't sheep country but the true farming destiny of the North Island was identified early. A correspondent in the *Maori Messenger* in 1850 wrote:

The Northern Island of New Zealand is peculiarly adapted for

John Godley, an Anglican High Church Irishman, was the leader for the first two years of the Canterbury settlement. He was a director of the New Zealand Company and managing director of the Canterbury Association. Godley and his family sailed for New Zealand in 1849 to prepare for the arrival of the first ships. He returned to England where deteriorating health curbed what would probably have been a distinguished career. His eldest son, John Arthur Godley, became Secretary of State for India and was raised to the peerage as Baron Kilbracken.
(Alexander Turnbull Library, F-5079-1/2)

dairy farming. Its pastures are rich and nutritious in a remarkable degree. There is ample sufficiency of moisture throughout the year to sustain and nourish vegetation . . . the Tamaki meadows have throughout the year maintained 100 oxen on 100 acres . . . New Zealand might profitably become the dairy farm and market garden of Australasia.

The trouble was that wool could be shipped around the world but butter and cheese were perishable. Dairy exports to Australia from Auckland earned £850 in 1852, using salt and other techniques to give them a limited life. That was half as much as the export revenue from kauri gum and one-third as much as from potatoes.

Auckland grew as fast as it needed to, well away from the kitset colonies of the New Zealand Company. But throughout the North Island the clearing of dense bush and running-sore disputes with Maori over land ownership made development expensive and problematical. It wasn't until the next century that the north came into its own as a primary producing powerhouse.

※   ※   ※

The settlement that got closest to Wakefield's model was probably Canterbury. It wasn't a full cross-section of English society but it had the smartest and wealthiest middle class and did attempt to replicate an Anglican conservative establishment with High Church Irishman John Godley as its chief administrator. Given that Christchurch was surrounded by plains of native tussock, it was inevitable that wool growing would give the region an early economic boost. Land was cheap, much of it bought or leased for a song. Sheep from Australia cost around one pound a head. An estimated 100,000 sheep were grazing the Canterbury Plains in 1854 and half a million four years later when almost all the land had been settled. By then, about a quarter of a million sheep were on runs in Otago. Shrewd stationholders more than doubled their money in the 1860s. Then the profits declined. For example, Samuel Butler, later a famous writer, moved onto Mesopotamia in 1860 and cleared out four years later with double his investment. His timing was excellent, even if accidental.

My father – son of an indentured Scottish carpenter – used to say no one undertook the arduous sea journey under sail to New Zealand in the early days of settlement because they were doing well in Britain. Many left in hope but the arrival was often a shock. When my great-grandmother arrived to find Dunedin a rude, tiny clutch of shanties nestled precariously against gloomy bushclad hills, she and her female travelling companions sat on the beach and cried, as dolorous as the Dunedin drizzle, until they were lifted away by the men.

Many of the settlers defied this theory. They were well-educated young men, some with significant capital, who came out not because they weren't doing well at home but for adventure or to make their fortune, or both. Take Butler, an intellectual staked by a father who was glad to see the back of him. He took the money and ran. Take James Edward Fitzgerald, an Anglo-Irishman, who was in his mid-thirties when elected first Superintendent of Canterbury Province under the 1852 constitution. He was a graduate of Christ's College, Cambridge, a fine writer and excellent orator who played a part in provincial and national politics for many years. He stayed in this country to die in Wellington at the age of seventy-nine. Although hardly an international centre of culture and in many ways an ersatz England, Christchurch had the nearest thing to a highly educated middle-class society in those early New Zealand years.

But among this class too were some escaping their origins, some of the men my father had in mind. Every sheep station had its often romanticised tale of educated upper-class men among the workers. Some binge-drank their wages or seemed in their isolation to carry some secret shame beyond alcoholism. In some cases they received remittances from Britain to keep them buoyed financially. They were the sort of men who peopled the pages of John A. Lee's *Shining with the Shiner* and others of his stories of swaggers. The swagger,

James Edward Fitzgerald, an Anglo-Irishman, was elected first Superintendent of Canterbury Province while in his mid-thirties, and continued to play a part in provincial and national politics for many years. Cambridge-educated, he worked for the antiquities department of the British Museum before joining the Canterbury Association and emigrating to New Zealand on the Charlotte Jane, one of the first ships. Fitzgerald, the foundation editor of the Lyttelton Times, was a skilled writer and fine orator.

95

as no one of my generation needs to be told, was an itinerant worker, or tramp, who gained his name from the swag, or bundle of personal possessions he carried.

✿ ✿ ✿

Dunedin was more Scottish working class, and it was led by two much older men: the Rev. Thomas Burns, a narrow-minded, 52-year-old nephew of the great libertine poet, Robbie; and William Cargill, a former captain in a Highland regiment of the British Army, a more relaxed man who was in his sixties when he became Otago's first provincial superintendent. William Pember Reeves in *The Long White Cloud* said of 'the stiff-backed Free-Churchmen' who colonised Otago:

> Such men and women might not be amusing fellow passengers on a four-months sea voyage – and indeed there is reason to believe they were not – but settlers made of such stuff were not likely to fail in the hard fight with nature at the far end of the earth; and they did not fail.

A New Zealand Company surveyor, Frederick Tuckett, chose and bought the site for Dunedin. The favoured site was Lyttelton, then known as Port Cooper. Tuckett, a tough and unsociable man, explored a huge area of the South Island and recommended a change of site to Dunedin, mainly because it had more timber available for building.

Tasmanian-born Gabriel Read was the man who triggered the Otago gold rush with his discovery of large alluvial deposits at Tuapeka. A veteran of the Californian and Victorian fields, Read arrived in Dunedin in 1861 and fossicked around Central Otago after hearing that traces had been found there. Working with a spade, tin dish and butcher's knife alongside the Tuapeka River, he gathered two hundred grams of gold in a few hours. Instead of staying and amassing a personal fortune he advised the Otago Provincial Council that gold was present and plentiful. A rush to Gabriel's Gully helped end the economic slump that had gripped the province. Read then seemed more interested in teaching other miners the techniques of prospecting and in persuading them to settle any differences than in making his own fortune. He was later granted £1000 by the provincial government in recognition of the prosperity his discovery had brought to Otago.

The Scots applied themselves dourly to hard work and education. They were wary of what would happen to the Calvinist life they had quickly established when gold was at first rumoured – at Mataura – as early as 1856. Other traces were found in the deep alluvial valleys that slash through the big buckled backblocks of Otago, but these rivers were coquettish with their wealth until Gabriel Read, a Tasmanian-born prospector with experience on the goldfields of California and Victoria, made the first big strike near Tuapeka, in 1861.

Dunedin was only thirteen years old and nothing the Scots could do could keep the hordes from elsewhere in New Zealand, and from Australia and North America, at bay. The population was 12,000; ten years later it was 60,000, the biggest town in the country. More than twenty-three million pounds of gold was taken during the rush.

In a typically hard-headed manner, the Scots capitalised on the situation. The invading miners, along with labourers and artisans, some on the rebound from the goldfields, needed feeding and so did their horses. Arable farming boomed. By 1870, 800,000 acres were under the plough, almost all of it in the south, and a heavy engineering industry was established to make agricultural machinery. This tempo increased during the seventies when the area under cultivation increased fourfold to four million acres, and sheep numbers grew from ten to thirteen million.

It is worth reflecting on the relatively orderly behaviour of gold-miners in Otago and later on the West Coast. At the height of the rush, the population at the Central Otago diggings was an estimated 24,000, three-quarters of them miners. Although they were rough, macho communities, they never approached the lawless violence of the Victorian goldfields which culminated in the battle between police and miners at the Eureka Stockade.

Gold was first discovered in New Zealand near Thames in the Coromandel in 1842, but the amount taken was small. Small but payable finds of accessible alluvial gold were made at Collingwood in 1856 and in Marlborough in the 1860s.

In the mid-sixties, alluvial gold second only to Otago in quantity was found on the West Coast, a region which had been bought by the government from Ngai Tahu for only £300 at the beginning of the decade. This rush attracted thousands of miners who packed ships that rode the westerly across the Tasman from the declining Victorian fields. For many of the ships it was their last journey as they came to grief on the sandbars that a littoral drift deposits across the mouths of West Coast harbours.

The presence of gold in deep quartz veins in Thames was confirmed in the 1860s, but it required heavy machinery, and thus capital, to get it out; so it became a corporate industry.

Gold nowadays is still taken in small quantities in Central Otago, the West Coast, Southland and, on a larger scale, from the Martha Mine at Waihi. It has not been a significant export-earner for New Zealand for a long time but in the big production years of the 1860s, before meat and dairy produce were exportable, gold gave the country a phenomenal boost, and made Dunedin the economic capital of the colony. As it petered out, wool again became king of the exports, with what they called 'bonanza wheat' and other cereals significant earners.

Chapter Ten:

FROM BUST TO BOOM

A MONG THE MOST influential figures in nineteenth-century politics was Julius Vogel, journalist, businessman, and pre-Keynesian primer of booms by borrowing. He was twice Premier but it was as Colonial Treasurer in William Fox's administration at the end of the 1860s that he began a programme of development borrowing from overseas that totalled a staggering twenty million pounds over the decade. The money financed public works and an immigration programme (32,000 migrants in the peak year, 1874) which provided the labour and the population mass to develop an infrastructure: 1100 miles of railways, roads, bridges, port facilities, public buildings, and 4000 miles of telegraph.

This wonderfully creative economic thinking opened up large areas of hinterland and placed the country in a strong position when recovery came from the subsequent Long Depression. The trouble was that it caused the depression in the first place, or at the very least prolonged it. A recession occurred as the goldfields petered out in 1869, followed by a mini-boom as the Vogel plan kicked in, followed by the longest economic depression New Zealand has experienced, beginning in the late 1870s as wool prices began a long, slow slide.

Here is the scenario in the 1880s. The population of England had more than doubled to thirty-five million between the

Julius Vogel was Premier from April 1873 to July 1875 and from February to September in 1876, and was Deputy Premier in two administrations to Robert Stout. But it was as Colonial Treasurer under William Fox from 1869 that he launched a pre-Keynesian, pump-priming economic policy that resulted in borrowings of £20 million from overseas to finance immigration and build roads, railways and other public works. The scheme proved too rash and his popularity declined as the country slipped into depression. At the end of the 1880s, he returned to London and died there ten years later. Vogel was born in London and emigrated to Melbourne in 1852 where he became a journalist. The Otago gold rush drew him to Dunedin at the beginning of the 1860s and, with a partner, he founded the Otago Daily Times. Vogel wrote two books: A Handbook of New Zealand (1875) and a utopian novel, Anno Domini 2000: or a Woman's Destiny.
(Parliamentary Library, painting by William Menzies Gibb)

end of the eighteenth century and 1880 while livestock figures and food production hadn't changed much. Sheep in New Zealand numbered thirteen million and the local demand for mutton could be met by farmers on the edge of the towns. Cattle for beef became unsaleable. Getting rid of old livestock was a problem. The only way to ship surplus mutton across the world was by drying, canning, or boning and setting in barrels of tallow. Maori had preserved birds by storing them in their own fat for centuries but Pakeha hadn't noticed. The tallow technique was developed in Australia. A market existed for these products but it was at the bottom end because of problems of appearance and palatability, especially as the meat was from sheep bred to produce fine wool and not roast dinners or even stews.

New Zealand, contrary to the myth, was slow in developing techniques to preserve food for export, particularly refrigeration which rescued us from the prospect of perpetual peasantry. Australians built a freezing works in Sydney in 1861 and sent an experimental shipment to Britain under sail in 1876. It failed. Two years later they successfully shipped forty tons of frozen beef and mutton. That was a year after the first successful refrigerated cargo, from Buenos Aires to Le Havre. Not until 1882 did the *Dunedin* leave Port Chalmers with 5000 frozen sheep's carcasses which sold in London for £4000, about twice the price they would have fetched at home. Ten years later, more than a dozen freezing works were in operation.

It took dairying longer. Dairy farmers were clustered around the towns on undercapitalised family units with a few acres of quality grassland, some fences, a few cows and a shelter to milk them in. Once refrigeration opened up the prospects of

The Dunedin *sailing from Port Chalmers on 11 February 1882, with the first cargo of refrigerated meat for Britain. She arrived in London on May 24 and the cargo of 4908 sheep and lamb carcases was taken to Smithfield market that night for sale the next day. The return was double what the meat would have fetched at home. The success of the shipment changed the face of agriculture in this country. Sheep breeds developed to produce both wool and meat. The dairy industry moved from home to factory production. Refrigerated trade also turned New Zealand into an off-shore farm for Britain.*

large international markets, they had to set up butter and cheese processing factories as co-operatives and take their milk daily over the terrible roads in the high-rainfall areas of Northland, Taranaki and Waikato. The quality of milk varied and it took some time for a system to develop of regular milk supply to factories with financial incentives to keep milk quality high.

From the 1890s, the New Zealand economy grew on a very simple template that was to remain basically the same until the 1960s. Pasture became, as it remains, the most important crop. The grass-fed sheep were bred to produce fat lambs and coarse wool. A predominantly Jersey (much later, Friesian) herd was developed to produce milk for processing into butter and cheddar cheese. It took a few seasons for farmers to get the lamb cross-breds right for both meat and wool; and until government-sponsored meat inspections systems were set up, the quality was variable. But even then, meat quality was essential to meet competition from Australia and Argentina. Getting a high enough quality of butter and cheese to match competition from Denmark and Canada also took time.

Successive governments supported educational and

Dairy farmers began milking house cows by hand in open paddocks. Then, as they began sending milk or cream to factories, they built shelters. Next, before the middle of the twentieth century, came the widespread use of machines set up in 'walk-through' milking sheds. This enabled two or three members of the family to milk fifty or sixty cows, then an economic herd. This picture shows a 'walk-through' shed with machines but the farmer is hand 'stripping' each cow into a bucket after the milking-machine cups have been taken off. This was to ensure no milk was left in the udder.

research institutions to enhance the efficiency of this easy-care pastoral system. Research focused on the growth, nutrition and management of pasture; on sheep and cattle breeding towards high-producing animals; on the mechanisation of dairying from milking-machines to processing plants; and on the quality-testing of produce. Working within this narrow range of activity, New Zealand scientists and technicians led the world for the first two-thirds of the twentieth century.

A huge advantage was climate. Stock could stay outside year-round while an evenly spread rainfall kept the grass growing in many regions. Only small amounts of winter feed crops were needed to get animals through the short, slow-growth months. Without the need for wintering barns, farmers needed minimal capital compared with most pastoral countries.

Marketing was equally simple – meat, butter and cheese were sold in bulk to meet a mostly strong demand in Britain. Governments and producers often interfered in the marketing to get the best deal by restraining producers from competing with each other, and to manage returns in a way that levelled out the inevitable peaks and troughs in commodity prices.

In the 1870s, a change began to take place in the demographics and thus the politics of the colony. A relatively small coterie of educated people still held power, helped by plural voting based on property holdings. But former governor, George Grey, reincarnated as a democratic politician, and a group of other Leftish MPs formed a Liberal Party and won power. For a decade radical ideas had been simmering away such as support for industrial trade unionism, franchise for men without property requirements, votes for women, equal representation for Maori, free elementary education for all (passed in 1877), and pensions. Harry Atkinson was no radical but he embraced wide government intervention into public welfare, including an elaborate pension scheme to provide for orphans, widows, and covering sickness and old age. The pensions were rejected, even ridiculed, by his colleagues. Vogel set up the Government Life Insurance Office and the Public Trust Office. The Post Office Savings Bank had begun business in 1867. So the burst of radical legislation from the Liberal Party in the 1890s didn't come from nowhere.

Vogel's migrants poured in and swelled the number of working-class and lower middle-class people in the population. Grey remained an unreconstructed autocrat, opinionated and difficult and couldn't glue people together; so despite his advanced ideas, his leadership failed. His government fell in 1879 after a vote of no-confidence, but the party won the subsequent election for a brief period in power. In this election a town and country split appeared for the first time, and it endured for many years in New Zealand politics.

The 1880s were confused and unhappy for New Zealand. The Long Depression overlapped the end of the seventies and the beginning of the nineties and those migrants who had arrived in hope hung on in despair. Although land development and settlement continued, the depression had a devastating effect on national morale. Those who could afford to, emigrated to Victoria, New South Wales and the United States, resulting in the first European population decline since before the Treaty of Waitangi. Unemployment and poverty changed the attitude towards public policy. Opinion shifts towards the left also followed revelations of gross exploitation by employers of women and children, and incompetent and fraudulent business practices within the Establishment which brought down financial institutions.

As more people arrived under Vogel's scheme, land hunger grew, an appetite not unnoticed by politicians. By the end of the 1880s, large-scale farms, covering huge areas particularly in Canterbury and Otago, were held by a small number of owners. The Liberal Party, which came into office

Harry Albert Atkinson headed five administrations between September 1876 and January 1891. They were for short terms, except the last in which he was Premier for three years from 1887 until he was toppled by the Liberal Party in 1890. During his thirty years in the House of Representatives, he held a number of ministries. He was a brusque man, more admired than liked, but he adopted a number of liberal causes, some of which foreshadowed advances made by the Liberal administration that succeeded him. Atkinson was born in Cheshire, England, and emigrated to New Plymouth where he became an outstanding soldier in campaigns against Maori, for a time as commander of the famed Forest Rangers.

103

John McKenzie was Minister of Lands in the Liberal administration of the 1890s, and introduced legislation to break up the large sheep stations and to put small farmers on the land. One measure that reflected his antipathy to landlordism included an obligation for farmers to live on their land and improve it. The son of a poor Scottish crofter, McKenzie worked as a shepherd before coming to New Zealand. He was a station manager for South Island entrepreneur Johnny Jones before going farming on his own account near Palmerston in Otago. He entered Parliament as an Independent in 1881 but later joined the Liberal administration. He was a stalwart and popular man who fought with courage for the things he believed in.

in 1890 under John Ballance, had just the man to deal with the problem: John McKenzie, a Scot with a graphic memory of how the closures in his homeland had driven the people from their traditional land. Legislation while he was Minister of Lands helped break up the big estates by introducing a land tax and leasehold measures and by providing the government with the right to buy land under certain circumstances. Also built into the revolutionary measures were obligations to live on the land and improve it – a gesture against the absentee landlordism of McKenzie's Scottish childhood. A comment relevant to issues alive today was made by historian Tom Brooking in the *New Zealand Dictionary of Biography:* 'The 1892 Land Act made the notion of the Queen's chain more explicit than any other piece of legislation: McKenzie wanted all New Zealanders to be able to fish the rivers, lakes and coasts and to enjoy unrestricted access to forests and mountains.'

McKenzie also enacted legislation that enabled the government to buy more than a million hectares of Maori land during the 1890s, an action harder to understand in the light of his Scottish background.

✿ ✿ ✿

The townies bore the brunt of the Long Depression. Many believed they were leaving poverty, labour exploitation and landlordism behind when they sailed for their new country. But the governing elite was not going to give up easily and the practice of ministries reshuffling many of the same men continued through most of the eighties. But among them, as the decade closed, were men of the future, including John Ballance, Robert Stout, Richard John Seddon, William Pember Reeves and Joseph Ward. Ballance was elected to lead a new Liberal Party which was to transform politics and society.

The old order clung to three advantages. First was the plural voting. That was steadily being dismantled. Second was the 'Country Quota' which had become law in 1881. It based rural electorates on a third less population than urban electorates, thus enhancing the power of the farming vote. It was cut to eighteen per cent in 1887, raised to twenty-eight per cent two years later, and not abolished until 1945 to save the Labour Government from defeat in the 1946 election. Third was the Legislative Council, packed with old-guard members appointed for life. It killed progressive legislation, and an aristocratic and snooty Governor-General, the Earl of Onslow, tried to stop the Liberal Government from appointing new and sympathetic members. Ballance appealed to the British government and Onslow's successor was instructed to approve the new Prime Minister's appointments.

🌿 🌿 🌿

In other parts of the New World, settlers were disillusioned that excesses of capitalism had followed them from the Old – especially the aggregation of land ownership. Millions of working class and lower middle-class people read and

William Pember Reeves was a devout Fabian socialist who became Minister of Education and Justice, and later of Labour, in the Liberal Government that won the general election of 1890. He became famous beyond New Zealand as the architect of legislation to improve conditions for workers, to encourage trade unions and to make court arbitration compulsory to resolve disputes between employers and employees. His ideas were rather too radical for the pragmatic Seddon and he was packed off to London in 1896 as Agent-General. Reeves was born in Christchurch, was an outstanding scholar at Christ's College, and played both rugby and cricket for Canterbury. He worked as a shepherd before qualifying as a barrister and solicitor, and then was Parliamentary reporter for the Lyttelton Times, of which he was later the editor. He entered Parliament in 1887. Reeves was an outstanding writer producing what may be called a New Zealand classic, The Long White Cloud, in 1898, and State Experiments in Australia and New Zealand in 1902.

absorbed the theories of utopian socialists such as the American, Edward Bellamy. In most countries they dreamed of change. But in New Zealand they got it – from the Liberal Party, elected to power in 1890, about the same time as the number of New Zealand-born Europeans first outnumbered the foreign-born. It was also the first one-man-one-vote election with every male over twenty-one, with or without property, eligible to vote in the electorate he lived in. When women were enfranchised three years later, it became one-person-one-vote.

The government passed a range of humane and innovative laws. Among those that had the greatest impact were the introduction of an old-age pension; a full franchise with votes for women; graduated taxes on land and on income; a radical set of protective laws to enhance working conditions and encourage trade unions, including compulsory state arbitration between employers and employees; and free places in secondary schools. Families were encouraged onto small farms, especially in the North Island where the bush was being cleared. The government didn't shy away from state intervention or control and took over the Bank of New Zealand when it faced failure. The State Fire Insurance Office was set up to compete with private insurance companies.

So a number of influences had come together. The electorate was radicalised by the massive migrations of the seventies and the desperate depression of the following decade. The franchise was extended and, very significantly, the elite, landed gentry rule had come to an end. This shift was even more dramatic with the elevation to Prime Minister of Richard Seddon on the death of Ballance in 1893. Men like Ballance, Pember Reeves and Joseph Ward were fairly urbane men of the left but the rambunctious Seddon was loud, garrulous and uncouth. He was capable of gross grammatical solecisms, and dropped his hs from where they should have been and hitched them where they didn't belong. The broad accents of his birthplace, St Helens in Lancashire, were hardly at all smoothed by living in New Zealand. A big, very strong former West Coast publican with a stentorian voice and enormous stamina, he enjoyed eating and drinking so much that when he travelled the country it was considered useful lobbying to hold a banquet for him.

On the other hand, Seddon also had a profound and useful knowledge of parliamentary procedure and tactics, an ability to hector or cajole people into line as he needed to, and an extraordinary astuteness in gauging what the electorate wanted and giving it to them as though he'd thought of it first. Among the cooing of Liberal idealists, his was a pragmatic voice. His party hesitated at electing him on Ballance's death. Most wanted Robert Stout to lead but he wasn't a member of the House of Representatives at the time. One who would have liked the job was Pember Reeves – a man so different from Seddon it is hard to imagine any area of personal compatibility. New Zealand-born and one of the best and most versatile writers of his day, Reeves was a Fabian socialist and proud to proclaim that. Keith Sinclair suggests that the early big fights with conservatives were about land and tax policies and Seddon took care of those. Reeves' trail-blazing labour laws raised hardly a voice in opposition. Any further radicalism by Reeves, though, would have taken the party too far to the Left. Although Seddon certainly had real sympathy for the working class, he knew the limits of the electorate's tolerance.

After a brief failure of nerve, Seddon seized the moment, and assumed leadership of the party. He gradually achieved a dominance over his cabinet and the country that has seldom been matched in New Zealand, earning him the soubriquet King Dick, ironically at first perhaps but then admiringly. Reeves was eventually packed off to London as New Zealand Agent.

Seddon stands out as one of the most extraordinary personalities of New Zealand history. It could be said that most successful politicians since have followed a Seddon tradition: don't mess about with ideologies, be a strong, pragmatic, Mr Fix-it leader because that's what Kiwis like. As Seddon's biographer R. M. Burdon said of him: 'Thought was a necessary prelude to action, but thought for its own

Richard John Seddon has a place in history as perhaps the most colourful and dominating personality ever to hold the office of Prime Minister. He came to power in 1893 on the death of John Ballance, and consolidated his grip on the leadership of the country as 'King Dick' until his death in 1906. A loud, domineering but shrewd and charismatic man, he had a rare understanding of how Parliament worked and what the electorate of his time wanted from its government. Born in Lancashire, Seddon worked as a farmhand and iron foundry apprentice, emigrated to the Victorian goldfields, followed gold to Hokitika, again failed as a miner and went on to become a storekeeper and publican. He was elected MP for Hokitika in 1879, represented Kumara from 1881 to 1890 and then Westland for the rest of his life.

107

Robert Stout was Premier for three years from 1884, and was Chief Justice from 1899 to 1926. Some members of the Liberal Government wanted Stout as Prime Minister when John Ballance died, but he had lost his seat in 1887 and no way could be found to get him back into the House before Richard Seddon claimed the prize. He later became MP for Wellington, but by then Seddon's position was entrenched. Stout was born in the Shetlands, was a teacher and a surveyor before leaving for Dunedin in 1864. He qualified as a barrister and solicitor seven years later, became a member of the Otago Provincial Council in 1872 and an MP three years later.

sake was mere idle indulgence.' He took up the catchcry that this was 'God's Own Country' and seemed to sit on the right hand of the Lord. He won five elections with ease, helped by the fact that the country became more prosperous every year and because New Zealand society was admired internationally for its egalitarian prosperity, and for policies that launched the world, for better or worse, on the road to the welfare states that proliferated in the twentieth century. Foreign politicians flocked here to look, and thousands of migrants came to live. Britain's two most famous socialists, Sidney and Beatrice Webb, visited in 1898, and while they admired much of what they found, even in Seddon, he was distressingly vulgar to their socially elevated taste.

The Liberals were lucky. Soon after their election prices for commodities began rising in Britain, easing New Zealand out of the depression. The optimism and confidence Seddon left behind him was immense. This was reflected in a number of books written in 1908 about their country by New Zealanders such as Robert Stout:

New Zealanders who visit the birth-places of their ancestors complain there is not the same joyousness in the homeland that there is in these islands . . . It is suggested the greater social freedom, the greater comfort, and the sunny skies are the cause . . .

And:

Utopia has however not yet been established in New Zealand . . .

James Cowan, in a book to celebrate a visit by American Navy battleships, a paean to the country's prosperity and progress, wrote:

Judged by the test of accumulated wealth, New Zealanders are in a more prosperous condition than any other civilised people on the face of the globe.

The Liberals lasted until 1912, led by Seddon for thirteen years until his death in office in 1906 at sea returning from a visit to Australia. William Hall-Jones was a caretaker for two months, followed by Joseph Ward for five years, and Thomas Mackenzie for four months.

Ward, a businessman, had had to leave Parliament at one time because of bankruptcy. His government experimented with the only variation on first-past-the-post elections before MMP in the 1990s. In the 1908 and 1911 elections candidates had to achieve an absolute majority in their electorates, if necessary by having a run-off election between the two top candidates seven days after the general election. He was an able, articulate man but had none of the charisma of Seddon, nor the party management skills. The Liberals were gradually splitting between the radicals who began looking to the burgeoning Labour Party and conservatives who found more in common with the Reform Party led by William Massey.

Ward was unable to glue the disparate groups together. He was briefly Prime Minister again, through 1929, as leader of a refurbished Liberal Party, renamed the United Party.

Joseph George Ward held a number of senior posts in the Ballance and Seddon administrations and was Prime Minister after Seddon died in office in 1906. He led the Liberal Government until 1912. He was later, briefly, Prime Minister at the head of the United Party in 1929. Ward was born in Melbourne, moved to Bluff as a child with his parents, was Mayor of Bluff on two occasions, entered Parliament in 1887 and held the Awarua seat until the first election after World War I. He re-entered Parliament in 1925 and resigned owing to ill-health in 1930. He was an able and articulate but uninspiring politician.

New Zealand early in the twentieth century was still essentially a rough, masculine pioneering society. The 1905 All Blacks who visited Great Britain and had been beaten only by Wales during an arduous tour had confirmed the general belief that the strong, silent colonial country men were the hardiest Britons of them all.

Getting by often called for a hardiness of spirit. The bush was still being beaten back by settlers, most of them with insufficient capital. The big estates, especially in the South Island, had long boasted large houses, and some colonists (which was the name used mainly for the relatively few moneyed settlers) brought in kitset houses from England. Most newcomers, however, lived in primitive houses, especially small farmers breaking in land.

The New Zealand Company provided immigration barracks at each of their settlement areas in the early days for communal living until settlers could provide for themselves. Some brought tents and set them up on arrival.

In many places, Maori built their raupo whare with the raupo reeds plaited and woven together and attached to posts and rafters, some with wooden doors and framed glass windows. They looked fine but they were usually draughty unless lined with calico, and the risk of fire was so great that cooking had to be done outside.

Permanent homes in the South Island were often made from cob. Walls were of mud reinforced by flax or tussock grass and rammed inside frames, or of cob bricks made separately. The trick was to get the roof right and to get the inside walls papered to prevent fine clay dust from pervading the house. But in most parts of the country wood was the readily available building material and two-room sawn-timber houses with laundry and toilet facilities in rickety outhouses were common – if not for the first house then for the more permanent dwelling.

For the small farmer, the house could not take up too much time because breaking in the land was the next priority. The bush was slashed and burnt and seed put down, usually for a brilliant initial crop spurred on by the fertilising ash. The bush was so cut back by 1900 in many areas that reforestation became a matter of government concern.

Remoteness was still a problem for many. In the South Island distances between properties were often great and in the North Island the crumpled landscape and heavy bush created a distance of its own. The Main Trunk railway didn't get through from Wellington to Auckland until 1908.

A middle class gradually emerged, and its members built mostly villas with a central hall running from the front door, with rooms on each side, to a kitchen at the back. This was the most common design for both substantial houses and small cottages. The more expensive were bay villas with a bay window and a verandah at the front. They simply fronted the street or the road with little attention paid to siting for sun and view. These houses went up in small towns, on farms, and in the suburbs that were spreading out from the main cities as tram services expanded.

The Liberal Party under Seddon's shrewd, strategic leadership bestrode a broad middle ground of national consensus. But as the party lost its momentum the nation's political divide began to open. The Political Reform League was set up in 1905 to protect freehold land against the leasehold movement, and became a focal point for a wider range of conservative opinion. The party gained support also from those who were offended by the Liberal Party's corrupt patronage of the public service that had grown under the glad-handing Seddon. On the other side of the crevasse about the same time, trade union leaders formed a Political Labour League and later a Federation of Labour in which many of the leaders of the Labour Party government of 1935–1949 began their political careers.

Of the two groups, the trade union-led workers' movement, backed by middle-class socialists, was the more vociferous. Its members believed the arbitration system Reeves had so proudly established the previous decade was not giving them a fair share of the national wealth, and some unions withdrew from registration, convinced they could do better with direct action. The Opposition coalesced in the Reform Party around Massey in 1909 and the following year the first New Zealand Labour Party was formed mainly by trade unionists.

A year after Massey became Prime Minister in 1912, battle lines were drawn. First miners went on strike in Waihi, and then a waterfront dispute led to a general strike which lasted for a month. The strike failed and many of the leaders of the defeated 'Red Feds' turned their attention to national politics as a better means to achieve their ends. But the rifts that already existed between town and country and rich and poor were ripped open wider when young farmers, sworn in as special constables during the strike, attacked workers. 'Massey's Cossacks', as they were tagged, created a bitterness that hung around for more than twenty-five years.

Among the strike-breakers was a young dentist, Bernard

111

Freyberg, who would be involved in a far greater calamity than a strike that awaited the country: in August 1914, World War I broke out and New Zealand agreed to send an expeditionary force to help Britain.

Chapter Eleven:

WAR AND PEACE – OF A KIND

A S MY PEREGRINATING parents traipsed me around the country as a small boy, I became aware of obelisks, often set in the centre of a town intersection, and sometimes seemingly nowhere, alongside lonely roads, perhaps not far from a country hall to suggest some bygone hamlet. They bore the names of those killed in World War I, as few as ten or twelve and as many as fifty or sixty. I was struck by how many of the remembered dead on quite small memorials had the same surnames – brothers and cousins from nearby farms. These monuments were silent reminders of the consequences in these distant settlements of the madness that afflicted Europe in the second decade of the twentieth century. The New Zealand civil wars of the nineteenth century constituted a greater national disaster, fought as they were on home ground, but at least they had a point to them – one side trying to keep its land and mana, and the other trying to take the land and subjugate the native culture. Whereas it is hard to define any human or divine, good or evil purpose to the world war that consumed so many lives all those years ago.

World War I was New Zealand's greatest catastrophe of the nineteenth century. In one day at the Battle of Passchendaele in 1917, 640 of its soldiers were killed and 2100 wounded. That came after the eight-month Gallipoli campaign of 1915, during which 2721 were killed and

4752 wounded. The war erupted from political tensions within Europe and settled into attrition between lines of trenches and bunkers, with the British (later helped by Americans) and Germans each making ferocious forays at what seems now to be an insane cost.

Prime Minister William Massey said on the declaration of war: 'All we are and all we have are at the disposal of the British Government.' Military training had been compulsory in New Zealand since 1909, which meant sufficient trained men were available to despatch a force of 1400 to occupy German-administered Samoa eleven days after war broke out, and to send 7000 men to the Middle East less than two months later. New Zealand's sacrifice from 1914 to 1918 was exceeded in the Empire only by Britain. From a population of one million one hundred thousand, 102,000 served overseas, which included about fifty per cent of the male population aged between nineteen and forty-five, and 1500 nurses. The official death toll on active service was 16,554 but another 2000 died directly because of the war, and nearly 50,000 were wounded (many of them twice or more).

As the war ended, an influenza epidemic cast a shadow over the world. It arrived in New Zealand in October 1918, like divine retribution among civilians, and within three months had killed more than 8500 people.

I was struck by how many of the remembered dead on World War I memorials had the same surnames, brothers and cousins. The memorials are still silent reminders of the consequences here of the madness that afflicted Europe in the second decade of the twentieth century.
(George Adkin photograph, Te Papa Tongarewa, Museum of NZ)

New Zealand responded with alacrity to the 1914 British call to arms because of an informal agreement that had existed since the 1880s. The Royal Navy would provide a defensive cover for the Pacific colonies in return for a financial subsidy to the Royal Navy, the provision of naval bases and an undertaking to provide soldiers for imperial wars. But there was more to it than that. God, Queen and Country patriotism still had a hold on the people. Public statements at the time and letters home from soldiers make it clear the glorification of dying in war for a British race of inherently superior morality and civilisation was still a powerful force. The letters, particularly, are testimony to how different a world it was before the 1920s.

The war became purposeless, was prodigally wasteful of young men's lives, achieved little, and left Europe in turmoil. It is a platitude to say a New Zealand identity was forged on the anvil of Gallipoli, but that gallant defeat certainly changed New Zealanders' view of themselves. Kiwis fought on Gallipoli with Australian forces, as the Australia and New Zealand Army Corps, and the day they landed on the beaches, April 25, became and remains Anzac Day, the focus for lamenting war dead in both countries.

For decades before the war, New Zealanders had an amalgam of beliefs – some of which seem contradictory now – that made them jingoistic and imperialistic. In the blend were a smugness that this was a better environment to live in than Britain, that they were more ruggedly independent, practical individuals, imbued with superior common sense. This was overlaid by a self-consciousness, a deep insecurity, about whether these virtues outweighed a lack of what they assured themselves were the effete qualities of cultural sophistication. Self-confidence burgeoned with international praise for progressive social legislation, with the acknowledged admiration for the New Zealand soldiers in the South African War, and with the impact of the 1905 rugby team in Britain and its surprising superiority over Britain's best.

So Britons were great but New Zealanders promised to expand their virtues in their Pacific paradise. From the beginning, they saw an imitation Britain of the south – the sincerest flattery indulged by any member of the Empire. So leaders wanted to take up a kind of franchise to civilise savage nations nearby, building up an empire of their own. Governor Grey had asked the British government in 1848 to enable New Zealand annexation of Fiji and Tonga. Twenty-three years later, Julius Vogel had sought the annexation of Samoa. He foresaw the day when New Zealand would have dominion over all of Polynesia. It was even put to the Americans that Hawaii should belong to New Zealand. One of the reasons they didn't sign up to an Australasian federation in 1901 was their belief in an inherent superiority over Australians with their convict origins. In that same year, Britain gave over the Cook Islands and Niue, but balked at any further colonial aspirations.

New Zealand was the first colony to sign up for the South African War – even before it started. Some sympathy was expressed in Britain for the Boers, but very little in this country. During the 1899–1902 war, 6495 New Zealanders served in South Africa, of whom 228 died, fifty-nine in action and the rest of wounds or disease. In one of the most disastrous battles Kiwis ever fought, at Bothasberg in 1902, twenty-four were killed and forty-one injured from a force of eighty.

The red, white and blue jingoism was not without a tint of paranoia, understandable in a small, sparsely populated island half a world away from its mother protector, but inexcusable in its extremes. The 'Yellow Peril' fear was always hanging in the air; a Russian scare caused the jitters in the 1880s; followed by a German scare and then desperate social unease at the presence of Dalmatian gum-diggers in Northland. Richard Seddon was loudly part of this. He not only trumpeted patriotism, but was scathing in his contempt for the Chinese and he attacked the 'Dallies'.

The Dalmatians, or Austrians as they were called, first arrived as early as 1858 and a wave came in the last two decades of the nineteenth century. The clannishness that made them so successful at exploiting kauri gum provoked suspicions that led to Royal Commissions into their economic and social effect on Northland, in 1893 and 1898. The investigations found more to admire than to disparage. Nevertheless, the Kauri Gum Industry Act of 1898, which allotted certain gum reserves for 'British' diggers was a flagrant move to restrict Dalmation immigration. Their numbers by then totalled about 1500 in the Auckland province.

It wasn't as direct a device as the 1898 tenfold increase of the £10 poll tax which had been imposed on Chinese in

1881. Other moves against Chinese followed even though their numbers were decreasing. Indeed, poisonous chauvinism led to the murder of a Chinese resident of Wellington by a mad racist called Lionel Terry, and to a speech Seddon made in Rarotonga when he said Cook Islanders would be better off with the bubonic plague than Chinese immigrants. (A New Zealand case of the plague had caused its own extravagant fears in 1900.) It was an introverted, paranoid 'White New Zealand Policy'.

As late as the 1920s, E. K. Mulgan, a senior inspector of schools in Auckland and his writer son, Alan, included in a book called *The New Zealand Citizen* a passage on immigration as follows: 'We want immigrants but we do not want everybody. We do not want the destitute, the criminal or people belonging to the coloured races. The experience of the United States of America, where millions of Negroes and people of mixed race form one of the gravest social and political problems of our time, has made us determined to keep New Zealand white, though we make an exception in the case of Maoris, whom we treat as equals and admit to citizenship. It would take too long to tell you why we keep out people belonging to coloured races, save to say that it is a question of ways of living and ideals, besides, of course, the desire to keep the blood of our people pure.'

Although New Zealand delegates blustered their independence at the many Commonwealth conferences held during the first half of the twentieth century, governments showed no great desire to cut the umbilical cord. A large measure of internal control had been adopted since the 1850s, but governments seemed reluctant to make the final gesture towards nationhood. Following Dominion status in 1907, the Governor became the Governor-General – and little else changed. The Statute of Westminster ended any control over the Dominions in 1931, but it was voluntary and New Zealand didn't bother to invoke it until 1947. *God Save the Queen* was the national anthem until 1977 when *God Defend New Zealand* was given equal status.

Many New Zealanders called England 'Home' until after

World War II. Such 'nonsense' surprised and amused George Bernard Shaw when he visited in 1934. Locals also referred to the ships that plied products and people between Britain and New Zealand as 'Home boats'. This was because the emotional ties were reinforced by the economic – the two economies were virtually meshed until the 1960s, with New Zealand an offshore British farm, and Britain an offshore New Zealand factory. This arrangement brought a high level of certainty and prosperity to New Zealand – apart from some small bumps in demand and supply, especially immediately after the war, and during the serious Depression of the 1930s, which affected every Western country.

William Ferguson Massey was Prime Minister from 1911 until his death in 1925. He was always juggling disparate groups in Parliament to retain power and never had a substantial majority – a tribute to his tenacity and political skill. Massey (seen here with Lady Massey) rallied conservative opinion within Parliament under the aegis of his Political Reform League so well that he became Leader of the Opposition in 1903. His gradual ascendance began as large property owners became increasingly uneasy about the growing militancy of Labour and the support for leasehold among Liberals. Massey was born in Londonderry of Scottish stock, the son of a tenant farmer who emigrated and took up leasehold land at Tamaki. He worked first for his father and then for John Grigg at Longbeach Station in Canterbury. After he returned north he became MP for Waitemata in 1893 and then in 1896 successfully stood for Franklin, a seat he held for the rest of his life. He was stolid, puritanical, an unquestioning believer in the virtues of the British Empire, reviled by many, but a symbol of good order to others.

The man who presided over New Zealand during the turbulent years of industrial strikes, a long harrowing war, an epidemic and a brief post-war recession was a burly Auckland farmer, William Ferguson Massey. Not only did large outside events press on his administration, the Reform Party's control of parliament under his leadership was always tenuous. During the war, Massey was forced to share power with the Liberals in a national coalition. The Deputy Prime Minister and Finance Minister was Liberal Party leader Joseph Ward, a Catholic. Massey was an Orangeman and a Mason. These attachments at that time ensured a bleak relationship.

Surmounting all the difficulties that dogged him would have crushed the spirit and curtailed the career of a less able and tenacious politician. The son of a tenant farmer, 'Farmer Bill', as he was dubbed, was born in Londonderry, Ireland, and came to New Zealand at age fourteen. Unfortunately, he brought with him some of the bigotry and hatreds that flourished in his home region. Massey worked for his father on a leasehold farm near Mangere. Later, he moved to the famous Longbeach Station, near Ashburton, the property of New Zealand's most innovative and famous farmer of his time, John Grigg. Grigg had been a neighbour of the Masseys in Auckland for ten years after arriving from Cornwall in 1854, but had decided prospects were better in Canterbury. Massey came back to Auckland to his own leasehold farm and entered Parliament for Waitemata in 1894. The Liberal Party was ascendant, but his self-belief was strong and gradually he became the major spokesman for the small, fragmented right-wing groups.

During the opening decades of the twentieth century, the number of farmers grew steadily as dairying developed into one of the three major export industries. Thousands of men went onto small properties, cleared the bush and developed dairy herds. Unlike the sheep farmers, they were up from nothing, but they shared some of their conservative values, especially a contempt for soft urban workers and their radical politics. An argument that had been stewing away for many years was between the Liberals who supported the leasehold of land and conservatives who believed more stoutly in the concept of private property and thus campaigned for freehold. Massey emerged as leader of a Reform Party that believed in freehold land, in preferential treatment for the rural industries and in the stern application of law and order at a time of increasing unrest among urban workers with their clamorous but uncoordinated desire for change.

The North Island population passed that of the South in 1901, a trend that continued and accelerated during the century. That shifted political power north as well. Some farmers' sons from the south moved to the areas opening up for dairying in Taranaki, Northland, the Waikato and the Manawatu. The value of butter and cheese exports more than trebled to three million pounds between 1900 and 1910 and nearly trebled again by 1920. North Island land settlement was almost complete by the time the government provided incentives worth about twenty-two million pounds to place returned servicemen in homes and on farms in the 1920s. Some took on land with insufficient economic potential and after a few bleak years walked off it. Others, by bidding for existing farms, used their government backing to borrow heavily and this edged up land prices, already judged by economists to be unrealistically high. When downturns in commodity prices came during the 1920s, the heavily indebted cow cockies, as they were colloquially called, struggled to stay afloat. When the big Depression hit in 1930, the government had to help to prevent thousands of farmers from losing their properties – although banks and loan companies couldn't have sold many of them anyway.

Dairy farmers were the navvies of the industry. Oliver Duff wrote in 1940:

> . . . the battle of the sheep and the cows, if it is not the battle of two civilisations, is the battle of two social systems. Sheep make gentlemen and cows unmake them.

Most dairy farmers early in the century had too little capital to develop their land and equipment, and insufficient income to pay for additional labour. During the 1920s tractors and improved milking-machines became available and the value of superphosphate was acknowledged. But not enough small farmers had the money to join the technological advance. They and their families worked long, hard days – and seven of them in every week during the long summer season.

Life was especially arduous for farm wives, and many a country schoolteacher told stories of kids falling asleep in class – up since 5 a.m. and back to the milking shed for a couple of hours after school. With their growing numbers, the small farmers began to use their political clout more forcibly. Those who had previously given their support to the Liberal Party moved to Massey. Gradually, the farmer tail wagged the government dog and a lot of public money was spent on rural infrastructure. Businessmen, whose natural place seemed to be in Reform, were disaffected by this but politically they had nowhere else to go.

The Reform Party under Massey had little of the proud independence of the early Liberals who enthusiastically acknowledged their close relationship with Britain, but built a fence against interference with their internal affairs and pushed a foreign policy line of their own at Empire conferences. Massey and his colleagues put the New Zealand child back to the Motherland's breast. He believed in a kind of messianic role for the British Empire, made regular trips to England, and even became associated with the British Israelites, a fringe religious group that believed the Empire had a divine role to play in world affairs. He described the League of Nation as 'for fools . . .' and thought 'Dominion' too pretentious a name for the country when that status was granted in 1907.

But to the farmers, well, Massey was their man – stolid, conservative, orthodox, puritanical, a man reviled by many, revered by few, but a symbol of good order at a time when the towns and cities were rumbling with discontent at a diminishing standard of living. Pember Reeves's once-vaunted Arbitration Court had come down more often in favour of employers than employees. Some trade unions opted out of the system and took direct action. A railways workers' strike in 1924 was strangled and the following year Reform won its biggest victory with fifty-six seats in an eighty-seat House. But Massey didn't live to enjoy the luxury of an easily controlled Parliament. He died of cancer a few months before the election.

New Zealand is historically a puritan society, dominated by people with censorious moral beliefs. And liquor, they believed in earlier times, led to unrestrained self-indulgence – especially promiscuous sex and, thus, the breakdown of the family. A Prohibitionist leader,

The war for and against the outlawing of alcohol was fought with great emotion at all levels – on the streets through pro-prohibition protests and between intellectuals. The Professor of Mental and Moral Philosophy at the University of Otago, William Salmond, published a 67-page booklet called Prohibition, a Blunder *in 1911 and within weeks a fellow citizen of Dunedin, A. S. Adams, published a wordy rebuttal called* Professor Salmond's Blunder – Prohibition: an Effective Social Reform.

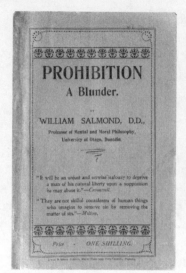
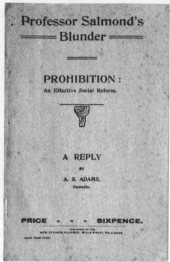

A. S. Adams of Dunedin wrote in 1911:

> This is not an inviting subject for the reader, but the open sore of the social body cannot be healed by plasters. One terrible fact in relation to the sexual evil is that drink is largely responsible for its prevalence.

So legislation was designed to keep alcohol away from the mingling of the genders. No more barmaids could be registered after 1911, at which time there were 1000 in the country. Over the years, ageing and arthritic barmaids became the only ones available. It was an offence to supply liquor to Maori women. In 1939, it became illegal not only to have alcohol at a dance but to have it 'in the vicinity of a dancehall'. Separate private bars or lounges were set aside in hotels for couples or women drinkers. As no man would be seen in one, and few women for that matter, they were almost always empty.

Robert Stout wrote in 1908:

> Has organised society a duty to look after the physical and moral well-being of [its] members? The New Zealand people through their parliament give an emphatic affirmative reply.

He was right. They had. Stout and his wife were avid supporters of the temperance movement, a cause that had first been organised in Hokianga a century earlier. Like all pioneering societies with a preponderance of men, New Zealand had a history of heavy, reckless drinking, and the problem was exacerbated by the especially high consumption of locally made whisky. The temperance movement gained added momentum when women, the main victims of drunkenness, were given the vote. After that, the drive for prohibition became the greatest, most emotional moral crusade in New Zealand history. In the 1880s, as it gained momentum, Thomas Bracken, author of the National Anthem, wrote a poem that began:

Thomas Bracken was the most esteemed New Zealand poet from the 1870s until the early twentieth century. His brief verse, Not Understood, was published as a booklet and became a standard work among those who recited poems in public. Bracken was born in Ireland, sent to Victoria with an uncle when he was twelve and an orphan. He worked on a sheep station before coming to Dunedin in his mid-twenties, in 1869. He was already writing verse, and after his arrival he turned to journalism. In the early 1880s, he entered Parliament for Dunedin and embraced policies that were very liberal for that time. His career in politics lasted only six years. Although his poetry is not now regarded very highly, he has enduring fame as the author of the National Anthem. In 1876, the New Zealand Saturday Advertiser published his poem, God Defend New Zealand, labelled it the 'National Hymn', and held a competition to set it to music. Judges ruled the score written by Otago music teacher John Joseph Woods as the winner. It was declared the National Hymn by the government during the Centennial celebrations of 1940. It became the National Anthem in 1977, given equal status with God Save the Queen.

> *False spirit! Take thy fiendish shape,*
> *Thy name is demon, and not wine;*
> *Durst thou sling to the purple grape,*
> *Durst thou seek shelter 'neath the vine?*
> *Nay, cling to thy patron – Death;*
> *And hide thee 'neath his blackest pall;*
> *Throughout creation's length and breadth,*
> *Thou are the vilest fiend of all.*

Not long before Bracken wrote this, Anthony Trollope had observed:

> I must specially observe one point on which the New Zealand colonist imitates his brethren and ancestors at home – and far surpasses his Australian rival. He is very fond of getting drunk.

The prohibition movement in New Zealand was noble in it intentions, pervasive in its political influence and negative in its social consequences. More than fifty years after it began

Grog's Own Country
by Conrad Bollinger
(1959), a history of
liquor licensing was a big
seller. Bollinger started
the book with: 'Most of
we New Zealanders are
fascinated with liquor.
We either disapprove of
it so strongly or enjoy it
so much that it forms
one of our favourite
topics of conversation.'

its crusade, drunkenness was as widespread as ever. In the mid-1950s, the annual per capita consumption of beer was just below 100 litres. But throughout the whole period, legislation against liquor marched unstoppably on. Prohibition orders could be taken out to stop excessive drinkers from drinking at all and to prohibit barmen from serving them; hours were cut back from 11 p.m. to 10 p.m. and then to 6 p.m. in 1917; a law against 'shouting' or 'treating' in bars was introduced in 1916 but was revoked as unworkable in 1920; and the issuance of licences for making or selling liquor was virtually halted. When a brewers' licence was issued to Dominion Breweries, the Women's Christian Temperance Movement held a prayer meeting in front of the new brewery at Otahuhu. With 'heads held high, shining eyes and an air of strong resolution and purpose', according to the *Auckland Star*, they asked God to turn it into a factory for food or clothing. That was in 1931.

The laws were often enforced, or over-enforced, according to the personal attitude of local police. A grocer was convicted in 1910 for selling 'Stearn's Wine of Cod-Liver Oil Extract', a 'flu prophylactic, because it contained eighteen per cent 'absolute alcohol'. The conviction was overturned on appeal. But in many parts of the country, police were tolerant of after-hours trading, with men skulking in darkened bars, usually served by the publican. Furtive entrance and hurried egress were frequently by side or back doors. Police would be forced to act if a wife complained that she knew her husband was drinking after-hours in a particular pub, but would often give the publican a telephoned warning to clear the premises before they arrived.

A 1974 Royal Commission on the sale of liquor said in its report:

> . . . the history of our liquor laws more than anything else represents
> a microcosm of New Zealand social history as a whole.

That was incontestably accurate. A Justice Department summary that same year divided the history of the legislation into five phases:

. . . a laissez-faire approach from 1840 to 1873, early efforts at
regulation from 1873 to 1893, a rising tide of prohibition and
restriction from 1893 to 1918, a long stalemate between 1918 and
1948, and a gradual trend towards liberalisation since . . .

One of the first measures by the General Assembly in 1852
was to exempt Parliament Buildings from sale of liquor laws.
But forty years later, the gathering power of the Alliance –
the organisation that represented the various temperance and
prohibitionist groups – cowed even the bibulous Seddon.
Advanced by what Wellington journalist Pat Lawlor called
the intemperance of the temperance movement, legislation
in the 1890s made the sale of liquor a local option. Many
towns and suburbs voted to be 'dry'. Prohibitionists were
convinced that without alcohol social problems would
disappear and a kind of communal bliss would prevail – much
as some people think today about illegal drugs. Indeed, the
Alliance used the term 'liquor traffic'.

The triennial vote on 'Prohibition' or 'Continuance' slid
steadily towards the former, up to 55.8 per cent in favour in
1908 – but a two-thirds majority was needed. Then, with
the rules changed and only a simple majority needed, in 1919,
Prohibition won by about 15,000 – before the votes of soldiers
overseas were counted. The soldiers, who had experienced
English pubs and French cafés and been lobbied in Europe
by visiting New Zealand brewers, voted four to one against.
The country was saved from the social disruption that
followed Prohibition in the United States.

From then the vote began to slide away from Prohibition
but political parties remained nervous of the power of the
Alliance. They continued to hold Royal Commissions of
Inquiry to get the problem out of their hair and stayed with
the regular polls rather than face the challenge of an election
with the broad-based temperance movement focused against
them. And they were wise to do so. In a referendum in 1949
on the simple issue of extending closing time from 6 p.m. to
10 p.m., 6 p.m. won with an ease that astonished everyone.
At the same time, referendums on Compulsory Military

Training and off-course betting on racehorses both effected change.

My father, a renegade from a Presbyterian family, was a moderately heavy drinker and after the referendum I asked how he voted. He said for 6 p.m. Even as a boy I realised that some of the old puritanism was lodged under his easy liberal veneer. Like many of the men who had all their adult lives staggered out of the pub at 6 p.m., he couldn't trust himself to resist pressure to stay on if the hours were extended. Typical of the puritan tradition, he was caught neurotically between the camaraderie of the public bar and the aftermath of guilt. The liquor industry didn't push too hard for later closing time in 1949 because they were making big profits under the heavily regulated regime. Beer consumption was high on world standards and the product was poured frenetically into the customers in a few brief hours a week. The head of Dominion Breweries, Henry Kelliher, a stout defender of six o'clock closing said: 'They may drink too much but at least they go home.'

The six o'clock swill was a mad daily hour between 5 p.m. and 6 p.m. when hundreds of thousands of men throughout the country, particularly on Fridays, packed into public bars to drink one of only four or five mainstream beers made in the country at that time. From the 1930s, the beers were manufactured in huge quantities by two major brewing companies. It was four per cent alcohol by volume, coloured brown and sweetened by caramelisation, and poured into jugs or glasses through portable taps on the end of long rubber or plastic tubes. The tempo of pouring and drinking increased as the clock moved onwards. When the pouring stopped at six, patrons had about ten minutes to consume what was left in jugs, a period established by a court ruling. During this period, drinkers were harassed by bar staff who had to hose down the premises before they could leave.

The stupidity was that the beer was not heavily intoxicating unless drunk quickly; so six o'clock closing, designed to curb drunkenness, ensured it. On the West Coast, after-hours drinking was endemic. Police virtually gave up

The six o'clock swill occurred during a mad daily hour when hundreds of thousands of men throughout the country packed into public bars to drink as much beer as they could between the end of the working day and closing time at 6 p.m.

on it. When ten o'clock closing arrived, some Coasters complained that they lost drinking time on Friday and Saturday nights when bars had kept serving behind closed doors until 11 p.m.

The swill continued until ten o'clock closing won a poll in 1967 – fifty years after six o'clock was introduced as a wartime measure.

Firm puritanical moral beliefs on right and wrong tend to push people towards excessive discipline and uniformity of behaviour. One manifestation of this was the Society for the Health of Women and Children founded in Dunedin in 1907 by Sir Truby King, a mental hospital superintendent. The name was shortened to the Plunket Society after the society's patron, Lady Plunket, wife of the then Governor-General. King's activities in the south brought about such a dramatic reduction in infant deaths that within a few years branches were established in every centre in the country. Soon the nation was trumpeting the lowest infant mortality rates in the world. Mothers and children to a remarkable degree followed a uniform regime of feeding, weighing and potty-

Frederic Truby King founded the Society for the Health of Women and Children, which became the Plunket Society, named after Lady Plunket, wife of the then Governor-General. The idea of setting uniform and disciplinary standards for the raising of children sat comfortably with the nation's puritanical moral beliefs and resulted in a dramatic reduction in infant mortality as the society's branches spread around the country. King was a New Zealand-born, Edinburgh-educated physician and psychologist who became Superintendent of the Seacliff Mental Hospital, north of Dunedin. His range of interests was extraordinary. He made contributions in the fields of alcoholism, nutrition, mothercraft, psychological medicine, and even plant nutrition and soil erosion. He spent several years helping the British set up a similar system of child care. When he died eleven years after retiring in 1927, he was accorded a state funeral, such was his fame and the affection the community felt for him. (Alexander Turnbull Library, S.P. Andrew Collection, F18662 1/1, photographer S.P. Andrew, 1938)

training their babies under the supervision of trained, registered Plunket nurses.

The effect was largely positive but in its passion for averages and for disciplined child development it left little room for the idiosyncrasies of individuals.

🐟 🐟 🐟

Although the British offshore farm model brought many years of prosperity, it made the country excessively vulnerable to twitches in the British economy. During the war, the government bought up farm production and sold it directly to the British government – an arrangement that meant New Zealand may have paid dearly in lives but a twenty-years-long economic boom continued. However, when the British economy turned down and prices dropped after the war, New Zealand had nowhere to hedge her bets. So the twenties didn't roar here, they meowed. Some years were better than others but uncertainty prevailed followed by a gradual decline. Then came what has been simply labelled the Depression, the deepest economic slump of the twentieth century.

The image of the New York Stock Exchange disaster in 1929 gives an impression that the Depression happened dramatically, as though our economy fell over a cliff. But signals began in 1926 when seasonal unemployment turned permanent, rising fairly steeply again in 1928, even though farming was expanding steadily as prices in Britain fell. Assisted immigration, running at about 10,000 a year, was suspended. The big shock did come in 1930, though, when export returns fell by more than half. And it got worse.

The Depression was traumatic for New Zealand as well as most Western nations. By the end of 1931, the number of registered unemployed approached 40,000, and thousands more were engaged on public works mainly financed by loans from Britain which dried up as the crisis continued. Two years later, came the nadir. An eight million pounds deficit loomed, and unemployed doubled to more than eighty thousand. Wages were cut by ten per cent. In some industries, staff worked one week in two. Many farmers couldn't meet mortgage payments, and the most indebted were forced to walk off the land.

The two administrations from 1925 to 1935 tried unrelenting deflationary measures: cutting taxes and decreasing expenditure to balance the budget. Pensions were cut and health expenditure reduced. The school entry age was raised and the exit age lowered, and teachers' training colleges were closed. Public service salaries were cut and public works cut back. The desired result was achieved. The budget was balanced – as the public looked on in misery.

A committee on unemployment, on which the Labour Party was represented, turned down the idea of a dole of the sort paid in Britain. Conferences were called of farming, business and banking leaders to seek constructive ways of levelling out the burden, and of keeping desperate farmers on their farms with various mortgage relief measures. But the only productive investment of taxpayers' money was in

Joseph Gordon Coates was Prime Minister for three years after succeeding William Massey as leader of the Reform Party in 1925, and he remained an influential and effective politician within the government coalition that ruled from 1931 to 1935. He later served in the war cabinet. Coates was born in Northland (1878), was elected the MP for Kaipara in 1911, won the Military Cross and Bar in World War I and served as a senior minister in Massey administrations. He was admired by his peers for his courage, his genuine compassion and his sense of duty.

grants to farmers and schemes to get more men on the land – in a world awash with pastoral products.

The dominant politicians through the worst years were Joseph Gordon Coates and George Forbes. Coates, MP for Kaipara from 1911 until his death in 1943, entered Parliament as an Independent Liberal. A farmer, he joined Reform because of his opposition to the Liberals' leasehold beliefs. He had a distinguished war career, became a cabinet minister in Massey's administration on his return in 1919 and Prime Minister in 1925 shortly after the death of Massey. His leadership was confirmed with a triumphant Reform Party win in the general election that year.

Coates was acknowledged by all as a brave and generous man who embraced no ideology. He alienated many conservatives with government intervention in transport, power generation and with welfare programmes such as a family allowance for families with three or more children. But it wasn't a good time to be Prime Minister as governments around the world fumbled for ideas to staunch the economic bleeding. Reform was well beaten in 1928 but Coates remained an influential member of a Reform-United coalition government under United leader George Forbes.

Forbes, also a farmer and one-time Canterbury rugby half-back, was a lesser man but held power longer. Almost every political commentator has made some sort of corny metaphor about him playing badly but behind a beaten pack of forwards. His Depression policies favoured forms of retrenchment, mostly modelled on British tactics. He had decided during a visit there that the dole was demoralising for those who received it, that no money should be given to anyone without working for it. But 'relief', as the work-for-dole scheme was called, was considered even more demoralising by those men from all walks of life who had to dig ditches through swamps, plant trees, plant maram grass on sand dunes, chip weeds from footpaths, and do other make-work tasks for seven shillings a day, ten for married men. The only daring if not desperate and not necessarily successful measures – such as devaluation and lowering interest on internal debt

– came from Coates as Minister of Finance.

New Zealanders lost much of the confidence in themselves and their country that they had built up over forty years. The 1924 All Blacks had reaffirmed their sturdy colonial physical superiority over the effete Old World, and moving pictures were a distraction in a country which had previously had little public entertainment. But, as the Depression deepened, many believed capitalism had failed. The prevailing monetary system needed to be abandoned and a new economic reality constructed for the benefit of all. They turned politically to the left, embracing communism or some other form of socialism. Others, especially groups of farmers, became adherents of new monetary systems, such as Douglas Credit (which became Social Credit in its reincarnation after World War II).

George William Forbes was Prime Minister for five years during the Depression of the 1930s until he was crushed by the landslide win of the first Labour government in 1935. Born in Lyttelton and educated at Christchurch Boys' High School, Forbes played halfback for Canterbury in the 1890s. He became MP for Hurunui in 1908 and held the seat until his retirement in 1943. He served as a minister in the Liberal administration of Joseph Ward and formed a coalition government with Coates's Reform Party in 1930. History sees him as an honest but unimaginative man.

Theories based on a conspiracy of financiers to bring down the economy for their own advantage proliferated. Sadly, even the Old World paranoia against a mythical Jewish conspiracy raised its bestial head here. Anger grew among the poor and unemployed and flared occasionally into violence. The most serious outbreak was Auckland's Queen Street riot of April 1932 in which unemployed grappled with police. Windows were broken and shops looted.

The nadir years were 1932 and 1933. After that, export revenue began to grow, first from big increases in wool and then meat prices. But it was too late for Reform or United. The Labour Party swept to power in 1935. They had been gaining votes over more than twenty years but, because their support was generally confined to the largest urban areas, the number of seats they held in the House of Representatives fluctuated. Their leaders had shed policies the cautious New Zealand electorate considered too radical. They seldom talked any more about the socialisation of the means of production, distribution and exchange, or the nationalisation of land.

In 1933, Labour's long-time Parliamentary leader, Harry Holland, had died. He was a self-educated Australian political journalist who arrived in New Zealand aged forty-four on the eve of the Waihi miners' strike, and became editor of the

influential trade union newspaper, *The Maoriland Worker*. Holland – twice jailed in Australia and once in New Zealand – was a tough-minded ideologue who believed capitalism would crumple in a class war and be replaced by socialism. The Depression was a fertile field for him to till in speeches and articles but his record suggests he may have been too inflexible to have been a successful Labour Prime Minister. That role was taken by Holland's successor, a brewery worker from Auckland who had been successful there in local body politics, Michael Joseph Savage.

Henry Edmund Holland (Harry) was the first leader of the Labour Party but died two years before the party gained office in 1935. Australian-born (1868), he came to New Zealand in 1912, was editor of the Maoriland Worker, *fought conscription in World War I, became a West Coast MP in 1918 and remained in Parliament until his death. He twice went to jail for his outspoken radical views, twice in Australia and once in New Zealand. Holland was a clear and compelling writer as a journalist, poet and propagandist but it is likely that the first Labour government would not have been as successful had he been the leader because of his deep-dyed ideological beliefs.*

Chapter Twelve:

A NEW PROSPERITY

ON MY OFFICE wall hangs a photograph of Michael Joseph Savage – a bump of grey hair above his high, pale forehead, rimless glasses and a benign, yet prim smile that would grace the face of a sainted nun. Prints of this same photo once hung in tens of thousands of living rooms of ordinary New Zealanders. It was – to use accurately a word now mostly abused – an icon of the time. From the time he took office in 1935 until his death in 1940 at age sixty-eight, he was the most genuinely loved Prime Minister this country has ever had. His public image was created by speeches from the platform and on the radio, which was just becoming a powerful political medium. Those speeches, delivered with quiet humility, expressed his belief in the right of ordinary people to enjoy personal and social security. A favourite phrase was that the sweeping welfare provisions of his government in its first five years of office were simply 'applied Christianity'.

Savage's appeal was enormously helped by his avuncular appearance, that of a slightly bumbling, kindly man of the people. His death, not to put it too crudely, was timely for his image. He and the welfare state he had helped create were at the height of popularity. Conservative, pro-private enterprise thought was in hibernation following the Depression. The train bearing his body from Wellington to Auckland stopped at twenty stations on the Main Trunk line

Michael Joseph Savage, Prime Minister from 1935 until his death in 1940, was the best-loved leader in New Zealand history. The gentle and benign image that shines from photographs, which graced the living-rooms of thousands of New Zealanders in the 1940s, helped make him the most popular leader the country has ever had. Australian-born of Irish stock, he left school at fourteen and worked as a shop assistant, farmhand and gold-miner. In his early thirties, he moved to Auckland, following a Victorian colleague, Paddy Webb, who also became a major personality in the Labour movement. Savage worked as a brewery cellarman, stood for Parliament in 1911 and 1914 and failed both times, and joined the Labour Party on its formation in 1916. In 1919, he became an Auckland City Councillor and a member of the hospital board and then the MP for West Auckland, a seat he held for the rest of his life. He was deputy leader of the Labour Party from 1923 and succeeded Harry Holland ten years later. This photograph shows people mobbing Savage with congratulations after Labour won the 1938 election.

to allow people to honour him, before his long funeral procession bore him to the Savage Memorial on Bastion Point, jutting out into the Waitemata Harbour, the last great memorial to a politician in New Zealand. It is impossible to imagine a latter-day leader attracting such reverence, perhaps because the lives of modern politicians are so intensely scrutinised. In the radio age, listeners could not see the warts and all.

Benign though his image was, he was clearly no soft touch as a politician. Powerful forces, particularly the medical establishment, were confronted as Labour prepared its radical welfare policies. Savage had frequently chaired the fractious Labour caucus from his earliest days in Parliament. It took the eloquent, egotistical and ambitious John A. Lee to cower him, and that wasn't until he was ailing.

I bought my Savage picture cliché for a joke but I leave it there to remind me of a New Zealand that was bursting with energy, optimism and pride that lasted from this second coming of the welfare state until the 1960s, apart from the black hole of the 1951 waterfront dispute. The country was one of the wealthiest two or three in the world. After a Depression sandwiched between two gruelling wars, people everywhere were determined to make the world a better, fairer place to live in. Nowhere was in a better position than

New Zealand to make such a transformation. The economy grew stronger year by year from 1934, buoyed by growing export earnings, and a government was in power from 1935 that promised dramatic change towards a society free from material insecurity.

The Savage administration's Social Security Act passed in August 1938 was a spectacular advance towards a complete welfare state, giving every citizen a free health service from doctor visits to hospital care, including mental hospitals, and maternity services – provisions watched with varying degrees of admiration and alarm by radical and conservative interests in other countries, especially Britain, Australia and Canada. It was like an all-embracing, national Friendly Society. Indeed, it panicked Friendly Societies here and abroad who provided health benefits to members into redirecting their resources, often into Credit Unions. Legislation also extended and expanded pensions, including a universal old-age pension at age sixty-five. A massive state building programme made affordable, modern housing available for workers, and the government provided free milk for all schoolchildren. The Reserve Bank was nationalised, giving the Minister of Finance power over the banking system, and the State Advances Corporation, established in 1894, became an effective instrument for providing cheap loans to farmers and urban house buyers. The welfare state was a winner, as Labour's landslide win in the 1938 election demonstrated. Over the following years, other welfare provisions included a family benefit for every child, compulsory annual holidays with pay for all workers, and even free textbooks for schoolchildren. Long after Labour was out of office, until the 1970s in fact, successive administrations not only didn't openly challenge welfare, they often fought election campaigns on claims they had extended it – or would, given power.

Social Security was funded at first by a separate social security tax paid by wage and salary earners, but this was never quite enough so the fund was topped up from the Consolidated Fund. Eventually the whole cost was transferred to the Consolidated Fund. Income was taxed on a graduated scale which rose proportionately with income. Unearned income, as it was called, was often taxed twice – once through company tax and then as income tax by those who received dividends. Someone earning the equivalent of $2400 a year (a high salary then) paid twice as much as someone on $1200 who paid four times as much as someone on $300. What may seem extraordinary now is that this method of income redistribution to provide for a full range of social services was seldom even questioned as being less than just until the 1970s. Social security and the tax regime that supported it were based on the principle of egalitarianism which was certainly socially successful but has since been vigorously challenged as seriously detrimental to economic growth.

The dominant members of this fourteen-year Labour Government were Savage, Peter Fraser and Walter Nash. Savage and Fraser were the two Prime Ministers and Nash Minister of Finance, and Deputy Prime Minister to Fraser. Labour had had a solid core of MPs since the early 1920s, but a factor in keeping them from office was the ability of conservatives to scare the electorate by referring to the extreme radicalism in the early trade union careers of Harry Holland, Savage, Fraser, Robert Semple, Paddy Webb and other lesser members of the Labour caucus, most of them self-educated to a level that shamed many of their university-graduate contemporaries. Many had also been monetary reformists of a fairly extreme kind. The 'funny money' factor was present in New Zealand politics for fifty years, until the 1980s, and was always a worry to the Establishment and even to the middle class.

Men like Holland, Savage, Fraser, Semple and Webb had been involved in the 'Red Fed' (Federation of Labour) strikes before World War I and had loudly fought conscription, not because they were essentially pacifists but because they insisted 'capital' should be conscripted as well as men. Some, including Fraser, went to jail for their protests. Savage was against conscription as World War II approached and was still talking about the conscription of 'capital' – but this time to ensure those who fought would be amply rewarded by society on their return. Nash was a pacifist in 1914–1918.

Even in the run-up to 1935, conservatives were warning of radical chaos should Labour be elected, but once in government, Savage, Nash and Fraser proved to be financially so orthodox that Lee – with the backing at first of sophisticated, university-educated MPs who came in with the sweeping Labour victories of 1935 and 1938 – began to challenge them and insist on the issue of credit to pay for welfare and public works in place of borrowing. He was held off, although at one stage went dangerously close to commanding a caucus majority.

Savage distrusted Lee and refused to have him in his cabinet, which exacerbated the situation in caucus where Lee had control over the left wing of the party and where he continued to foment dissatisfaction in favour of more haste towards his version of socialism and against the caution of Savage, Fraser and Nash. After the dying Savage again ignored him for a cabinet appointment, Lee began a campaign against his orthodoxy but overplayed his hand with a pamphlet, *Psycho-pathology in Politics*, a trenchant attack on the Prime Minister's mental ability to discharge his duties. He was expelled from the Labour Party in March 1940, two days before Savage died of colon cancer – a disease which curtailed even more prematurely the career of that other spearheading progressive politician of nearly fifty years earlier, John Ballance.

Lee lost his seat in 1943. He was fond of saying, at least later in life, various versions of: 'If you're not a communist before you're thirty you've got no heart. If you're a communist after you're thirty you've got no brains.' It was a revision of what he probably heard George Bernard Shaw refer to on his 1930s visit, 'the hoary old platitude that unless a man was a revolutionist at eighteen, he would be a fossil at forty'. But in the context of the Labour Party, Lee's was a telling maxim. All the former firebrands had become increasingly

John Alfred Alexander Lee was one of the most remarkable New Zealanders of his time – borstal boy, convicted criminal, DCM winner in World War I, politician, social commentator, novelist and short story writer. Born in Dunedin, he worked in factories and on farms and served prison sentences before the war in which he lost an arm. He was a Labour Party MP from 1922 to 1928 and from 1931 to 1940 when he was expelled from the party. He formed the Democratic Labour Party but lost his seat in 1943. Despite his lack of education, Lee was a fluent and lucid writer and an indefatigable chronicler of events throughout his long life. He wrote more than a dozen books including an autobiographical novel, Children of the Poor (1934), which depicted the poverty and depravity of his childhood.

conventional as they aged. Savage, after most of his life as an adamant rationalist, returned to the Catholic Church in his last years. Fraser, the militant Red Fed and anti-conscription protestor thirty years before, became vigorously anti-Communist and the protagonist for Compulsory Military Training. Lee himself supported American intervention in Vietnam in his old age.

Lee was an immensely able man, flawed by vanity and an inability to compromise. From an impoverished Dunedin family, as a boy he had served time in borstal for theft, became a fugitive and then at age twenty was sent to Mt Eden prison for breaking and entering. He served in World War I, won the DCM and lost an arm. On his return, he entered politics with gusto. He was in Parliament briefly in the 1920s, held the Grey Lynn seat from 1931, and in 1938 won it by the biggest margin of any seat in history, reinforcing his ambition and buffing his ego. He was an exciting platform speaker, his back straight, black hair standing up from his head like brush bristles, waving the stump of his left arm. His stentorian delivery could project to the back of a hall better than a Shakespearean actor. He was an indefatigable journalist, and an accomplished writer of short stories and novels, much in the style of Jack London, one of his idols.

By 1938 Lee had written a book, *Socialism in New Zealand*, already extolling the virtues and achievements of the three-year-old government, of which he was Parliamentary Under-Secretary to the Minister of Finance. He proclaimed the coming of democratic socialism and declared: 'New Zealanders are ready for any economic heresy which will serve the community.' Well, Savage, Fraser and Nash didn't believe that.

Lee kept writing all his long life and, once he had outlived his enemies, he rewrote history to settle old scores.

It's worth pausing to consider the apparent dichotomy of the New Zealander at the time of this first Labour Government

– on the one hand accommodating the most politically progressive government in the world, and on the other maintaining a reputation for being deeply, even bleakly, conservative. From Friday night after the shops shut around 9 p.m., until Monday morning, only dairies remained open to sell specified consumables. Not only was there no café life, only a handful of restaurants existed even in the main centres, apart from hotels which were mostly considered too expensive. Only two or three small blocks of flats in each of the main centres housed mainly old people. Everyone else retired to a house and section in the suburbs for a round of weekend chores – mowing lawns, gardening, painting and fixing the car – broken possibly by a visit to 'the park' during the winter for Saturday afternoon rugby. Men and women dressed in drab uniformity and conversational brilliance was regarded as a form of 'showing off'.

Poet and essayist A. R. D. Fairburn, a commentator and unremitting critic of the conservative nature of New Zealand life, wrote in the early 1940s:

> We New Zealanders are one of the dullest, most stupidly conservative, most unenterprising races on this planet. By a long course of self-hypnotism extending over several decades we have persuaded ourselves of the opposite – that we are bold, enterprising, progressive, intelligent people, unhampered by the shackles of the past. The sooner we realise what damned nonsense this is the better for us.

He also wrote:

> I am, a good deal of the time, bored by the insipidity of our social life. We have a Mediterranean climate in the north of New Zealand, and I should like to see us embrace a much gayer and more spirited way of living than our present one.

Fairburn, Robin Hyde, Frank Sargeson, R. A. K. Mason, Denis Glover and others were fully rounded New Zealand voices. Most writers before their generation had been smitten from childhood with the Anglophilia rife in New Zealand through to the 1930s, when it began to diminish. It finally

Arthur Rex Dugard Fairburn was an influential writer and social commentator from the 1930s until his death at age fifty-three in 1957. Fairburn was a descendant of a missionary who witnessed the signing of the Treaty of Waitangi in 1840. Rex, as he was commonly known, was born in Auckland, and after a conventional boyhood and education, during which he excelled as a sportsman, he became an insurance clerk. He wrote prodigiously as a freelancer: radio scripts, poetry, satire and newspaper and magazine articles. Critic Vincent O'Sullivan wrote of him: 'He castigated the society he lived in, yet his commitment was such that criticism at times brought him close to the elegiac.'

Frank Sargeson was the most accomplished and best-known short story writer of his time. Born Norris Frank Davey in Hamilton, he qualified as a solicitor, visited Europe in 1927, and returned to New Zealand determined to make himself a writer. He lived in a bach on Auckland's North Shore for many years and became a mentor to a generation of young writers. Sargeson achieved a special New Zealand voice in his short stories and novels.
(Robin Morrison Estate)

passed away in the late 1960s when Britain made moves to join the European Common Market. Anglophiliac voices were still heard through the 1950s but in its late throes the condition had few spokespeople. Generally, though, the generation that matured in the 1920s and particularly the 1930s were sophisticated and forceful and wholly New Zealand in their tone. Those like Fairburn and Hyde, who were also journalists, had a new authenticity. Fairburn even had the audacity to write a satire about the beloved Savage: *The Sky is a Limpet, a Political Parrotty*.

Their take on the conservative nature of society was confirmed by visitors. The American historical novelist James A. Michener wrote in the beginning of the 1950s: 'Along with the Spaniard, he [the New Zealander] is probably the most conservative white man still living'. And yet New Zealanders showed none of the disregard of, say, the Spanish for many practical forms of innovation. Farmers snapped up tractors and if they couldn't buy machinery, they often made it, even invented smart, labour-saving devices.

One reason may be that while New Zealanders were by temperament conservative they didn't feel trapped, or even imprisoned, within a long, exulted history as Europeans did. But perhaps the best explanation of this dichotomy comes from Bill Pearson's 1952 essay, *Fretful Sleepers*, which is about pervasive puritanism. He accepted that puritans had what

Oscar Wilde called 'uncouth morals and ignoble minds', but defended one aspect of their attitude:

> The intellectual usually assumes that the worst enemy is puritanism: disinfect the snuffy tin-roof-chapel conscience, he says, and our way of life will flower. But this is questionable. The Puritanism of Littledene is not all debit. With the concern for our neighbours' morals goes a concern for their welfare. The gossips are at least interested in other people, they help them in sickness, help with one another's ploughing and shearing and harvesting
>
> ...

Littledene, by the way, is a little-known New Zealand classic written about the disguised town of Oxford in Canterbury by Hugh Somerset in the 1930s and reveals much of what Pearson means.

So progressive, 'applied Christianity' sits credibly alongside the constricted, puritanical lifestyle of the time.

Only six months before he died, on 3 September 1939, Savage joined Britain in the war against Germany. Although he had been sharply critical of British foreign policy on occasions, he announced on the radio: 'Where Britain goes we go, where she stands, we stand.' I was eight years old when war was declared. We were staying overnight in Waimate on our way to New Plymouth where my father had a job on the *Taranaki Herald*. He woke me up and gave me a long cuddle, explaining ominously that we were at war again, expressing in his long embrace the apprehension, the dread, of those who remembered the disaster of twenty years before.

New Zealand again responded with alacrity to the call from Britain to help fight another European war. Major-General Bernard Freyberg had been among 'Massey's Cossacks', on the opposite side of a bitter divide from Savage's successor as Prime Minister, Peter Fraser. But any past differences were put aside when the government chose Freyberg to lead a New Zealand division on the outbreak of war. A war

Bernard Cyril Freyberg was one of the outstanding soldiers of World War I, in which he won the Victoria Cross and a number of other decorations for bravery. He was commander of the New Zealand Division in the Middle East and Europe throughout World War II. He later became Baron of Wellington, New Zealand, and Munstead, Surrey, and was Governor-General of New Zealand from 1946 to 1952. From 1953 until his death he was Deputy-Constable and Lieutenant-Governor of Windsor Castle. Born in England he came to New Zealand with his family as an infant and grew into a tall, athletic, champion swimmer. His fearlessness as a soldier became legendary and he was admired enormously by the New Zealand troops whom he commanded in their finest hours in the North African desert. He would probably have been promoted to a higher rank in the British Army during the war had he not failed as Allied Commander-in-Chief during the Battle of Crete in 1941.

cabinet administration was set up early in Wellington, including members of the National Party, which had become the main Opposition. The arrangement collapsed within a few months. To include a wider range of representation, Labour then persuaded two members of the former Reform/United coalition government, Coates and Adam Hamilton, to join the war cabinet as individuals. They resigned from the National Party caucus.

Freyberg was given unusual powers by the government. He was authorised to keep his self-contained citizens' army intact and not have units hived off to other divisions. He was able to make decisions about how and where his division would be engaged, even though it was almost always serving under a corps commander from Britain or, in Italy, the United States.

In 1939, the regular army numbered 500 men with 9000 Territorials. Although 60,000 men volunteered to fight in the opening months of the war, conscription was introduced in July 1940. An advance party of soldiers left within two months of the declaration of war, and the First Echelon of 6000 men a month later. The Second and Third Echelons completed the Second New Zealand Division in Egypt not long before it was called to help the Greeks repel a German invasion. The courageous Greeks had themselves beaten off an attempted Italian invasion through Albania. It was early in 1941, and with Australians and some other British and Commonwealth troops, the New Zealanders fought in Greece, Crete and the North African Desert while Britain regrouped its armed forces after the disaster of Dunkirk and endured the Battle of Britain.

The Kiwis suffered hugely against the better equipped, highly professional German army with its panzer divisions and dominant air force. They effected a strategic retreat down the Greek peninsula, outgunned and without adequate airpower and were evacuated to Crete, leaving behind much of their equipment. They failed by a hair's-breadth to hold Crete against a German airborne invasion. It became one of the major 'if only' battles of the war, refought in dozens of books since. The battle pivoted around the disposition of troops for defence and the critical loss to the Germans of Maleme airfield.

More than 2000 New Zealanders were taken prisoner, although 5000 escaped to Egypt, again evacuated by the Royal Navy. The Germans suffered so many casualties, shot out of the air like ducks by weary, ill-equipped defenders, they never again tried an airborne invasion.

Freyberg's reputation as a corps commander was damaged by the loss of Crete in which his decisions on where to place his units in defence pivoted around the information he received. Any chance of his promotion was capped. However, he retained the affection and support of the division and his courage was never questioned. One of his officers, writer Dan Davin, wrote a short story after the war called *The General and the Nightingale*, illustrating Freyberg's calm unconcern for danger. Freyberg became Governor-General after the war.

It was in the desert war with no civilians to complicate the campaign that the New Zealanders came into their own. The trials of Greece and Crete had turned them into seasoned soldiers with only Australian and some British units having comparable experience against the Germans. General Erwin Rommel and his Afrika Corps aimed to capture the Suez Canal and went very close to defeating the Allied forces. The New Zealand Division escaped encirclement by the Afrika Corps which had lapped around them and was closing in. They broke out in a courageous, brutal night battle at

Mersah Matruh and then, as John Mulgan, a young New Zealander serving in the British Army, wrote:

> Through all the days of a hot, panic-stricken July they fought Rommel to a standstill in a series of attacks along Ruweisat Ridge. They helped save Egypt, and led the break-through at Alamein to turn the war.

John Mulgan was the son of writer Alan Mulgan. He wrote a novel called *Man Alone*, for a long time on every university New Zealand English course reading list. It was considered the story that captured the quintessential New Zealand male. A brilliant student, he went to Oxford in the early 1930s where he graduated with distinction and began work with the Clarendon Press. He began the war as a second lieutenant in the British Army and rose to the rank of lieutenant-colonel. He served in the Mediterranean region and wrote in his *Report on Experience* of meeting the New Zealand Second Division soldiers in the desert:

> It seemed to me, meeting them again, friends grown a little older, more self-assured, hearing again those soft, inflected voices, the repetitions of slow, drawling slang, that perhaps to have produced these men for this one time would be New Zealand's destiny. Everything that was good from that small, remote country had gone into them – sunshine and strength, good sense, patience, the versatility of practical men. And they marched into history.

Captain Charles Upham won a Victoria Cross on Crete, and a bar at Ruweisat Ridge, the only combatant in history to win two VCs. Michener in his essay on New Zealand in *Return to Paradise* suggested New Zealand could claim to have produced the outstanding soldier in each of the two world wars: Bernard Freyberg VC in the first and Upham in the second. Freyberg was born in England but emigrated to Wellington with his family at age two. As a young man he was New Zealand's finest swimmer. He served with the British forces in Gallipoli and won the VC in France.

After the war in the desert was won, in September 1943, the division moved to Italy where the Germans exploited

The cruiser Achilles, part of the New Zealand Division of the Royal Navy, took part in the Battle of the River Plate in the opening months of World War II, in which British cruisers fought the German battleship, Admiral Graf Spee, off the River Plate in South America. The German commander scuttled his ship. Achilles returned to Auckland soon afterwards and the crew paraded along Queen Street, Auckland, to public acclaim.

the natural defensive advantages available on the long mountainous peninsula to stall their enemy. Freyberg became increasingly protective of his men, some of whom had fought with him since the Greek campaign. The Kiwis were part of a large Allied army and fought on in Italy until they raced to secure Trieste when the Germans in Italy surrendered early in 1945.

New Zealand also played a part in the Pacific war, however, with the Third Division, formed in New Zealand and shipped to New Caledonia in late 1942. The division fought the Japanese in the Solomon Islands alongside Fijian troops who were led by Kiwi officers and non-commissioned officers. The Third Division was disbanded in 1944.

Hundreds of New Zealanders were serving in the Royal Air Force at the outbreak of the war and thousands more passed through a Commonwealth air crew training scheme in Canada. By 1945, more than 9000 had served in the RAF in bombers, fighters and transport aircraft in every theatre of the war. A staggering 3267 were killed. After the Japanese entered the war, twenty-six squadrons fought in the Pacific under United States command.

New Zealand sailors began the war with the New Zealand Division of the Royal Navy, and later in a new Royal New Zealand Navy. The cruiser *Achilles* took part in one of the early successful sea battles, against the German battleship *Admiral Graf Spee* off the River Plate in South America.

Achilles was later replaced by the *Gambia*. Another cruiser in the division, *Leander*, served in the Pacific from 1942 after fighting in the Middle East; and an armed merchantman, the *Monowai*, was on escort and patrol duties in the Pacific, along with a number of minesweepers.

The official estimate is that 194,000 men served in the army, navy, air force and merchant marine at home and overseas, representing about sixty-seven per cent of men aged between eighteen and forty-five. A total of 11,626 died. Nearly twice that many were wounded. Casualties were higher in proportion to population than in Britain, Australia and Canada. About 10,000 women served at home and overseas.

The war in Europe ended in May 1945, and Japan surrendered three months later after atomic bombs were dropped on Hiroshima and Nagasaki. A number of New Zealanders, some from serving units, were sent to Japan as J-Force during the post-war occupation, staying until 1948. By then the cost of the war was estimated at half a billion pounds.

Why did so many go to war from here to the other side of the world? No one can deny that adventure always attracts young men to war, as well as the curiosity to see the world that in those days seemed so far away. But unlike during World War I, the causes of which most of the combatants never really understood, an acceptance was widespread that Hitler represented a unique modern darkness. Of the young men about to leave, novelist Ngaio Marsh wrote:

> They find it difficult even yet to believe in a direct threat to this country's isolation. Why then have they enlisted? It seems that, to explain them, one must use phrases that have been used too often and too easily. It seems that one must say of these young men that they are about to fight for an ideal, and that ideal is freedom, the freedom of a Commonwealth of nations.

When the war was six months old New Zealand celebrated the centenary of the Treaty of Waitangi, which was regarded as the document that gave birth to the nation — but more symbolically then than now. Preparations had been made well before the war started. A Centennial Exhibition was held at Evans Bay, Wellington, and a series of books on achievements over the century, the *Centennial Surveys*, was published by the Department of Internal Affairs. The twelve books were written by leading writers, covering aspects of history as well as the Maori people, science, women, education, farming, politics, social services and arts and letters.

On Schools Day, 20 February 1940, children throughout the country were issued with a silk scroll, and my one, frayed at the edges and foxed, within a plain frame, hangs on my office wall alongside the Fraser portrait. The scroll reads: 'Soon after lunch you will hear from the platform a short address which should make you proud of our history and grateful for our priceless heritage. As you listen to it, we feel sure you will make up your mind to do your best in the future to prove yourself a good citizen of this Dominion, and of the great British Empire to which we all belong.'

The celebrations were held against the backdrop of the disasters New Zealand soldiers experienced in the early days of a war that affected the local population more directly than World War I had, mainly because it was more truly a world war stretching across Europe and Asia and into our own Pacific neighbourhood. The country was called upon to produce as much food as it possibly could, not only for Europe but for Allied servicemen in the Pacific region, including tens of thousands of Americans who trained in this country before being despatched to undertake the hazardous task of island hopping to dislodge Japanese occupiers. They suffered huge casualties in places such as Guadalcanal and Iwo Jima, leaving many grieving friends and lovers in this country as well as at home. After the war, many New Zealand women,

Six months after World War II began, the country found time to celebrate the centenary of the signing of the Treaty of Waitangi. Many long-planned events included a Centennial Exhibition in Wellington and the publication of a series of special books that looked back on our history. On Schools Day, 20 February 1940, every schoolchild was issued with a silk scroll, the same as the frayed copy I have kept since. It exhorted us to be proud of New Zealand and to grow into good citizens.

known as war brides, flew to the US to marry men they had met here.

Because of the need for food, from 1942 all New Zealand men between eighteen and sixty-five had to enrol for national service, and under an emergency manpower scheme could be directed to work in essential industries if required. Many farmers were asked not to volunteer for the armed services and were exonerated from conscription to keep production levels as high as possible. The Home Guard, in which those ineligible for the services trained for defence of the homeland, had an enrolment of more than 123,000 at its peak in 1943. After the Japanese entered the war, the New Zealand government was asked by Britain to leave the Second Division in Europe on the understanding that the Americans would provide protection. Australian soldiers, with their country closer to the Japanese forward thrust, were sent home.

Of all the firebrand socialists of the first quarter of the twentieth century, Peter Fraser was the one who most typified the classic transition from the left to the right. Born in Scotland, he plunged into trade union politics immediately after his arrival in New Zealand in 1911, won a seat in Parliament for Labour seven years later and began his slow shift towards the reactionary he became in the last few years of his life. Fortunately, cometh the hour cometh the man – he was at the peak of his powers during the war years, a moderate in most things, determinedly orthodox in his economic management. He became as effective a leader as the country has had. He was self-educated to the highest intellectual level, brave, a shrewd judge of character, and self-assured in any company. With a fedora covering wisps of hair, his small round eyes peering through rimless spectacles over a prudish mouth, he was tough and often authoritarian – but without charisma. Fraser ran the war with a small war cabinet, visited London and also New Zealand troops in whose care and treatment he took special interest after the

Peter Fraser was New Zealand's wartime Prime Minister. A smart, solid man without charisma, he was nevertheless one of the finest leaders the country has had. Here he is (right) being greeted by Labour Cabinet Minister Robert Semple on his return from overseas in 1946. Fraser gained office on the death of Savage in 1940 and reigned until 1949. He was born in Scotland, the son of a shoemaker and small landholder, and was an apprentice carpenter when he left for New Zealand in 1910 at the age of twenty-six. He worked as a labourer and watersider before becoming a trade union official, and entered Parliament for Wellington Central in 1918. Fraser was Minister of Education, Marine and Police in 1935 and also held the health portfolio as the government prepared to set up a free medical service. During the war he travelled extensively, visiting New Zealand troops, but also, as this country's mana rose, to accept honorary degrees from Aberdeen and Cambridge Universities and the freedom of nine British cities. A skilled, firm administrator who had a talent for picking reliable and talented advisers, Fraser's popularity waned in the post-war period. He died a few months after losing office in 1949.

disastrous campaigns in Greece and Crete. The remnants of the Reform and United parties which had been shattered by the Labour landslide in 1935 had coalesced as the National Party under Adam Hamilton; but he had fallen victim in 1940 to Sidney Holland, a manufacturer from Christchurch. Holland and his caucus agreed to the postponement of the general election due in 1941, but he fought for a wartime coalition government. Labour resisted a full coalition but invited Holland to join a special war cabinet, which he did in June 1942 after the Japanese entered the war. Labour kept control of domestic policy and administration. Holland lasted three months. He pulled out following disagreements on domestic issues, mainly over how the government handled a miners' strike. One of these issues – ironically in view of what happened nine years later – was what Holland considered repressive wartime censorship.

Fraser's stature grew during the war and afterwards he played a major world role in the formation of the United Nations as a respected leader of the small countries. This turned the international spotlight on him and his country.

But his health was failing. He survived the 1946 election with a majority of only the four Maori seats and then seemed to lose his drive. Industrial strikes became frequent, especially by waterside workers and coal miners. This nightmare for a Labour government with its roots in the trade union movement recurred and enabled a revitalised National to make capital from the inevitable economic disruption.

The support Labour had from small farmers had fallen away, and Fraser and Walter Nash refused to release the country from the grip of wartime restrictions, despite the narrow shave in 1946. Petrol and some commodities were still rationed and a range of price controls had been maintained. The fear was that a slump would follow the war, as it had in 1920. But this narrow stabilisation programme alienated all but the most loyal Labour supporters – and even their allegiance was strained as, with bitterly anti-communist rhetoric, Fraser embraced the Cold War. His outspoken support for compulsory military training helped it win a referendum.

Thus, Labour suffered a defeat in 1949, bringing Sidney Holland to power as Prime Minister with fifty of the eighty seats in the House of Representatives. The war was over, and it wasn't followed by a slump but rather by two decades of prosperity. The National Party had seized the political middle ground and it would hold it, with two brief interruptions, for thirty years.

Chapter Thirteen:

THE COLD WAR
BECOMES LOCAL

S IDNEY GEORGE HOLLAND was ambitious, energetic, bumptious, and had the sort of hair-trigger intelligence that made him an extraordinary sight-reader, admired by broadcasters, and enabled him to get quickly to the heart of complicated issues. But he was intellectually and emotionally shallow. In private, he was companionable and down-to-earth, and sometimes surprisingly vulgar. Although he had none of the charisma of Seddon and, later, Robert Muldoon, he projected the same sort of ordinary bloke, common-sense image, especially liked in rural areas and the white-collar suburbs.

Holland had campaigned for his Reform Party father, Henry, a one-time Mayor of Christchurch, and incumbent for ten years in the Christchurch seat Sid, as he was universally known, inherited in 1935. He had also been deeply involved in business organisations in Christchurch. He rose quickly in the National Party because he was an aggressive debater and because he arrived in Parliament without a past among those who had formed the unsuccessful, ineffectual conservative regimes during the Depression.

Holland defined himself politically not so much by what he was for as by what he was against – socialism, which he saw as a scourge moving around the world to obliterate the sturdy independence of character promoted by private

*Sidney George Holland,
Prime Minister from
1949 until 1957,
brushed civil liberties
aside to deal with the
industrial dispute that
started with a waterside
workers' lockout early in
1951 and lasted for five
months. He brought the
Cold War to New
Zealand. Holland also
left his mark on
constitutional history by
abolishing the Legislative
Council soon after
gaining power. He was
born in Canterbury, the
son of an MP and
Mayor of Christchurch.
He acted as his father's
campaign secretary and
organiser and then won
his father's Christchurch
North seat for himself in
1935. Five years later,
he assumed leadership of
the new National Party
that had risen from the
unsuccessful Depression
coalition of the Reform
and United Parties,
helped by the fact that he
was untainted by direct
association with the
Depression regime.
Leader of the Opposition
until he won the 1949
election, he was a
decisive administrator
and aggressive debater
but shallowly pragmatic.*

enterprise. He had, briefly, been associated with the New Zealand Legion, a near-Fascist right group. The welfare state wasn't applied Christianity to Holland, it was 'applied lunacy'. But once in government, National knew it could not abandon social security without facing political oblivion and fought elections partly on an our-welfare's-better-than-yours basis, alongside some emphasis on private enterprise. The new government moved to dismantle some of the regulatory measures, especially some price controls that had survived since the war. During his time as Prime Minister, he steadily reduced the number of items governed by import licensing.

One of the first moves driven by Holland was to abolish the Legislative Council. It had been stacked with sympathetic members over Labour's fourteen years of rule; so National appointed what was tagged the 'suicide squad' – enough newly appointed members to vote for the council's demise. An undertaking was made to consider alternative forms of an upper house, including an elected senate, but it came to nothing. Holland also agreed to allow a certain period to lapse between the introduction of bills and their passage into law – and that also didn't happen, for long anyway. New Zealand became a single-chamber Parliament.

🐟 🐟 🐟

For the militant unions with their many unreconstructed Communists, the move to the right after 1949 was a challenge to be taken seriously. They were powerful organisations, given compulsory unionism since 1936, and some of them, as well as Holland, saw the 1951 industrial calamity as an ideological clash, a battle in the Cold War.

In that heyday of unionism, opinion was most trenchantly expressed and action most unified where significant numbers of members gathered together at workplaces, available to be roused by informed and plausible leaders. Waterside workers assembled each morning at New Zealand ports in what were called donkey rooms, in which regular stop-work meetings were held. Many of their local and national leaders were experienced and accomplished stump speakers who could mould opinion and make a case for action. One of the best was the national watersiders' leader, Jock Barnes, from Auckland. Miners and seamen also had regular opportunities to come together at the workplace. In much the same way, cow cockies were the most united and strident of farmers in their political opinions. They were closer to their neighbours than sheep farmers, gathered at factories to deliver their cream each morning in the days before cream was collected from the farm gate, and afterwards met often at their co-operative company meetings.

In February 1951, the national Waterfront Workers Union called for a ban on overtime after an unresolved dispute with employers on whether a fifteen per cent wage increase ordered by the Arbitration Court should absorb or be added to an earlier increase. They were 'locked out' by employers claiming ships could not be worked in a forty-hour week. The wharves came to a standstill. Holland moved with some relish to break the unions as Massey had nearly forty years earlier. Using the Public Safety Conservation Act of 1932, the government declared a state of emergency, deregistered the union, took action against other supporting unions, and used servicemen and 'scab' labour to work the wharves. The rebel unions broke from the FOL which failed to back them and formed the Trades Union Council (TUC).

The government's prohibitions against freedom of speech and assembly and against access to a whole range of democratic rights were draconian. They shocked civil libertarians, drove some few moderates onto the side of the watersiders, and demonstrated to alert observers that, despite New Zealand's long tradition of political stability, democracy was more fragile than they had thought. A political divide wider than any since the strikes of 1913 and 1914 opened up between the striking unionists and government supporters. Violence occurred, especially between unionists and 'scabs', often down back streets or outside pubs, and a riot flared up between police and watersiders not long before the end of

Jock Barnes was leader of the waterside workers during the 1951 industrial dispute. One reason waterside workers had such a strong union, ready and willing to take industrial action, was that they met in donkey rooms each morning and could be addressed by persuasive speakers like Barnes.

Fintan Patrick Walsh was a seaman and trade union official who became a confidant of Prime Minister Peter Fraser and an influential adviser to the Labour government. He refused to support the militant unions involved in the 1951 industrial dispute, thus making it easier for the Holland government to hold out and win the long battle. Born Patrick Tuohy in Poverty Bay, he worked in the United States as a young man and was involved in extreme unionism there. He was a physically powerful man, became a foundation member of the Communist Party of NZ in 1921, but twenty years later had become staunchly anti-communist. He became reviled by the left in later years as a symbol of those who had 'sold out'.

the dispute, during a protest march in Auckland's Queen Street. Marchers attacked police with bricks and bottles.

At the human level, though, many who strongly disagreed with the watersiders' actions gave succour to those of them among their friends and neighbours who were isolated by law from financial assistance. Large sums of money were smuggled in from Australian unionists to help the watersiders and their industrial allies to hold out, but the rebel unions miscalculated their strength and completely misjudged the degree of public support they would attract.

The government set up separate localised unions at ports around the country and, after five bitter months, triumphed, called a snap election to validate its actions and in September won fifty seats to Labour's thirty.

The militant unions had been seriously weakened when their cause was abandoned by the moderate unions within the FOL led by Fintan Patrick Walsh. Walsh was a shrewd and ruthless former Communist who had gradually become a member of the Establishment and one of the most powerful men in the country. He formed a friendship with Fraser and in 1942 became a member of the Economic Stabilisation Commission which oversaw the conduct of the economy from early in the war until National defeated Labour. In 1951, the seamen's union of which Walsh was president defied him and joined the watersiders but he had cultivated the backing of the small clerical and craft unions within the FOL.

The government's actions during the dispute were unrestrained partly because it had read public opinion more accurately than the militant unionists. Most New Zealanders were sick of direct industrial action in general, of militancy by the watersiders in particular, and were susceptible to a fear of Communism which was played up at this time, the height of the Cold War. The Labour Opposition, led by Walter Nash, tried a win-place bet, arguing for mediation long after it had become a political impossibility. Nash didn't want to seem to abandon the militants and his natural bent for tepid demurring and ambivalence led him to say famously, in the heat of the battle, in May: 'We are not for the watersiders nor are we against them . . .'

🌿 🌿 🌿

The waterfront dispute was played out against a larger, hotter battle in the Cold War, fought in Korea where, in 1950, the Communist north, eventually aided by Chinese forces, had invaded the Western-orientated south. Six thousand Kiwis volunteered for what became known as Kay-force. An artillery regiment, and transport and signals personnel were sent. When the three-year war ended in an armistice, 3794 soldiers had served in Kay-force. Thirty-three died on active service, seventy-nine were wounded and one was taken prisoner. In the shadow of the war, in 1951, New Zealand, Australia and the United States signed the ANZUS alliance to increase security in the Pacific.

The war stoked the New Zealand economy, mainly because of the demand for commodities, particularly wool. Wool returns were so high the government held back some money from wool growers for a period because of the burst of inflation that would have followed the release of so much income in a short period.

Holland's mediocrity became more apparent as the decade progressed but National retained power by a diminished margin in 1954, despite balance of payments worries. Monetary reform still stirred in the bosoms of many voters, despite the welfare system. Social Credit, based on the old Douglas Credit, was given a political base after thirty years in 1954 and won eleven per cent of the total vote but no seats under the first-past-the-post system. The National Government hoped to destroy any public belief in what were labelled 'funny money' theories by setting up a Royal Commission on Monetary and Banking Matters in 1955. The commission came up with a huge report the following year, basically supporting orthodoxy. No one but economists took much notice, though, and the best years for Social Credit were yet to come.

Bruce Craig Beetham was the most successful of the many politicians who have embraced the need for reform of the monetary system. He was Social Credit leader 1972–86 and 1988–91 and MP for Rangitikei 1978–84. Other monetary reformers had become MPs but Beetham was an excellent organiser and articulate spokesman who lifted Social Credit to its highest levels of recognition. He was born in New Plymouth and was a secondary schoolteacher before he took up politics.

It reached its zenith under the leadership of Bruce Beetham who held the Rangitikei seat as an MP from 1978 to 1984. Although Vernon Cracknell had held the Hobson seat from 1966 to 1969, the party was much stronger during Beetham's tenure, largely because he had reorganised and revitalised it himself. In 1981, Beetham was joined by Gary Knapp who won the East Coast Bays seat on Auckland's North Shore, and the share of the vote soared past twenty per cent. In 1984, Beetham was unseated. Knapp survived though and was joined by Neil Morrison from Pakuranga. However, the party's share of the vote fell and it headed towards oblivion.

Holland's health declined and when he retired two months before the election in 1957, his deputy, Keith Holyoake, was handed the leadership as a political hospital pass. Times were good and the election campaign was something of an auction with both parties bidding for votes. Labour's gift of £100 tax rebate as the country changed from annual tax payments to a Pay As You Earn (PAYE) system was the top bid and it bought the election.

Walter Nash was a prominent political figure for nearly forty years, as Minister of Finance in the first Labour government, then Leader of the Opposition, and a one-term Prime Minister from 1957. Born in Kidderminster, England, Nash worked as a clerk and shopkeeper before emigrating at the age of twenty-seven in 1909. He was a Christian socialist, an affable, courteous man who was a fussy administrator, increasingly unable to delegate as he grew older. He was secretary of the Labour Party when he became an MP in 1929.

Seventy-five-year-old Walter Nash, a relic of the radical Labour Party of the 1930s, became the new Prime Minister. His administration inherited a sharp balance of payments crisis. Nash and his Minister of Finance, Arnold Nordmeyer, were aghast at the terms of trade running against the country on a river of imports. They decided on what at the time was a logical and effective economic response by cutting the purchasing power of the masses with hefty tax increases on beer, tobacco and petrol. The 'Black Budget', as it is still called, would have been a political blunder by any party at that time, but for Labour, hitting the simple pleasures of the middle and lower classes proved fatal. In 1960, Keith Holyoake won at a canter, with a large defection from the polling booths by disaffected Labour voters.

The foreign exchange deficit didn't last, but the Holyoake government did, aloft on the wings of prosperity. It didn't have to land until the end of the decade. By then, the prospect of Britain joining the European Common Market grounded many of the country's economic aspirations.

In the two decades after the war, New Zealand was one of the richest countries in the world and its citizens shared this wealth as a right through an egalitarian redistribution that had become taken for granted. Optimism for the future was at a level it is almost impossible for people in the twenty-first century to understand. The talk among educationists was about training for life rather than for vocation as computers and other clever, labour-saving technology pointed towards shorter and shorter working hours and more and more leisure. Predictions from around the world were that the most pressing need would soon be food. Newspapers editorialised that New Zealand was right to concentrate on the production, processing and bulk marketing of primary produce – activities at which its farmers so excelled – for both economic and humane reasons with so many of the world's people undernourished and with population likely to outgrow food production. In the immediate post-war years, the Archbishop of York, Dr Cyril Garret, joined a chorus, warning that 'before the twentieth century is over Britain might face a food shortage on a gigantic and unparalleled scale'.

During the 1950s and 1960s, a revolution changed almost every aspect of the way New Zealanders lived their lives.

The inventiveness of scientists and technicians during the war prompted a technological boom. Cameras and film reached new levels of sophistication. Jet aircraft and nuclear power were realities. Computers began to emerge from calculating machines. Radios were hugely improved and soon to become transistorised and thus small and portable. Motorcars were suddenly more efficient and cheaper as roads were extended and improved. Industrial chemists were producing a gradually improving range of fabrics for cheaper, easy-care clothing, and also plastics to replace heavy and unwieldy metals. One of the most extraordinary developments during the second half of the century was the sharp reduction in the time between a technological invention and its commercial application and availability.

A consequence was a revolution in travel, entertainment and the availability of inexpensive labour-saving devices for the home and the factory. Movies had provided romantic escapism since the 1920s but new techniques, including colour, saw them develop a new realism. Then television, long a dream of the future, became commonly available. From 1960, it put New Zealanders in direct touch with the world, in tune with the burgeoning youth culture that accompanied the election of young and stylish President and First Lady John and Jackie Kennedy in the US. When the Vietnam War became contentious, it pulled Kiwis into the worldwide protest movement.

By the 1950s, the state housing programme and cheap loans began to make up for a housing shortage that had developed over three decades. For the first time, workers had access to forms of credit that enabled them to buy now and pay later. The greatest impact on the family of all this was in the kitchen, the laundry and, well yes, the bedroom. When the first contraceptive pills emerged, sexual activity moved from procreation towards recreation for those who could shed the weight of moral pressure against it that had been applied for thousands of years.

During these two decades, families ceased to be tied to their home suburbs or regions, or even to their remote and isolated nation. Children raised in the first half of the twentieth century could, and did, play cricket on suburban roads after school, removing their apple-box wicket to allow the occasional car to pass. Streets were everywhere but cars were not. Now mobile families could make easy expeditions to other suburbs or towns to visit friends or relatives. Crime became easier as criminals could escape the scene swiftly and anonymously. In 1960, the first commercial jets arrived, and in 1970 the wide-bodied 'jumbo jets' dropped fares down further, bringing the world closer, cheaper. The traditional years-long OE (overseas experience) by sea to Britain was replaced by frequent sorties to a range of countries.

New Zealand's many fast-flowing rivers were a boon for cheap hydro-electricity generation. The Reform Government at the end of the 1920s had built generating stations, transmission lines and substations, and sold the power in bulk to city councils and power boards to deliver electricity to homes. Subsequent governments continued the programme; so by the 1950s, power lines had spider-webbed their way around the country. This readily available, cheap electricity not only increased production on farms and in factories, it powered new anti-drudgery devices in homes. Refrigerators, electric stoves, clothes washing machines and driers, radios and record players, vacuum cleaners, and, a bit later, dishwashers were soon regarded as indispensable household appliances, especially in homes from which women began to emerge every morning to earn a second income for the family. These appliances were suddenly mass produced, and were relatively cheap, but still beyond the ability of most people to buy them for cash from wages.

In the 1960s, trading banks were the most staid institutions in New Zealand's commercial sector. Branch managers regarded those seeking personal credit as supplicants and treated them accordingly. They provided home mortgage money only on the solidest collateral. The oft-told joke was that the only way you could get a bank loan in New Zealand was to prove you didn't need one. Almost everyone's first home was built with the help of a low-interest mortgage from the State Advances Corporation, topped off perhaps with a second mortgage from a life insurance company backed by substantial endowment and life policies as collateral. Building societies had a significant share of the housing market, especially for second homes, because State Advances lent mostly to first-home buyers.

To get turnover volume, retailers set up their own credit

systems, mainly lay-by and hire purchase. Lay-by provided for people who would select a product and then pay it off at a certain rate each week or month and take possession when the full price had been paid. This was mainly for clothing and small items, whereas hire purchase gave buyers the chance to take cars, refrigerators and washing machines home and pay them off over months, or usually years. This avenue of credit is wider than ever today with the full range of financial institutions backing it, but it was for thirty years about the only show in town for borrowers who sought consumer items.

Credit cards didn't emerge until the 1970s. Late in that decade, national hire purchase commitments totalled $375 million and the public was still signing up to more than 500,000 new contracts a year. Compare that with financial institutions: credit unions had $14.5 million on loan, trustee savings banks $5 million in personal loans and advances, the Post Office Savings Bank $8 million, the Public Service Investment Society $10 million, and advances on building society shares were $12 million. Personal advances by all the trading banks totalled $126 million, and by the emerging finance companies $115 million.

An inhibiting factor against any form of credit in the post-war period was a residual fear of debt from Depression days, reinforced by the sense of thrift as a moral force. Borrowing was traditionally the last resort of the wastrel, the dissolute, the recklessly improvident. The Auckland Savings Bank, in 1847, and the other regional savings banks were set up by businessmen to foster the virtue of thrift among working people, not to make credit available. Advice against borrowing was almost as common and as ominous as warnings against promiscuity. The parable of the Prodigal Son is an injunction against profligacy as much as an enshrinement of forgiveness. Benjamin Franklin's admonition in *Poor Richard's Almanac* was widely quoted: 'If you would know the value of money, go and try to borrow some; for he that goes a borrowing goes a sorrowing.' I recall interviewing Sir James Fletcher in the early 1970s and discussing with him the purchase by his company of Diners Card. He sniffed that he didn't have a credit card and his wife didn't believe in them. I emphasise this because today's credit industry represents one of the great moral shifts of modern times, greater than the attitude towards sex outside marriage.

Chapter Fourteen:

THE SUMMER AFTERNOON

WHEN HE BECAME Prime Minister again in 1960, Keith Jacka Holyoake was regarded as a bit of a fool, a fop, his New Zealand diction overlaid with a toffee-nosed southern England accent derived from elocution lessons as a youngster. He was the first Prime Minister subjected to the rigours of television coverage, and he came across as pompous. His detractors should have known better, though, by considering his career. The *New Zealand Herald*'s long-time resident cartoonist Gordon Minhinnick drew a Prime Minister choosing his cabinet and saying to MPs something like, 'And now for the agriculture portfolio . . .' Those present were diving under the table. Agriculture was then considered by politicians as tougher even than finance. Few ministers emerged from the experience without diminished reputations. Farmers had the best organised and fiercest lobby, one that no government could afford to ignore. To manage them a minister needed to assure them of their importance to both the government and the nation, to pacify them without indulging them too much and, when necessary, to out-tough them.

Holyoake managed this task with such quiet ease few seemed to notice. It was a rare gift. I once visited his office to find his principal secretary chuckling away to himself. When asked why, he told me that a group of farmers had assembled in the lobby for an appointment with Holyoake and their undertones made it clear they were going to take him severely to task. 'An hour or so later they left,' he said, 'without their metaphorical shirts, chastened and bemused, and wondering how it happened.'

Despite his public image, 'Kiwi Keith' survived for nearly twelve years. A joke of the time was that no one admitted to reading the scurrilous weekly newspaper *Truth* but it sold more than a hundred thousand copies, and no one admitted to voting for Holyoake but he kept winning elections.

Holyoake had no secondary schooling, although he took private lessons from his mother who had been a schoolteacher. He was one of a long line of Prime Ministers, from Seddon – with only three exceptions – to Norman Kirk whose formal education stopped at primary school. He began farming in Motueka, became well known as a sportsman and while still in his twenties was president of the Golden Bay Rugby Union and the Nelson Province of the Farmers Union. At age twenty-eight, he won the Motueka seat in a 1932 by-election for the Reform Party. He lost the seat in 1938 but from 1943 until his retirement in 1977, was MP for Pahiatua in North Wairarapa (where he was born). He was a brilliant politician, a pragmatist unburdened by ideology, a master of consultation and consensus, always listening, never overreaching with policies that could explode in his face.

All this meant that nothing much happened during the 1960s except by very small incremental shifts, as the country basked in prosperity with a self-satisfaction that turned into smugness. The Holyoake administration did, though, oppose the policy of allowing South Africans to disqualify Maori from touring All Black sides, and sponsored the Hunn Report which drew national attention to the social and economic

Keith Jacka Holyoake was Prime Minister briefly in 1957 and then for eleven years from 1960, and Governor-General for one term from 1977. He was the first leader to come under the scrutiny of television and despite a foppish manner survived because he was a tough, shrewd and smart politician. Holyoake was born in the North Wairarapa, began farming in the Motueka area where he succeeded as a rugby and tennis player, and cyclist. He won the Motueka seat for the Reform Party in 1932 at the age of twenty-eight, lost it six years later, re-entered Parliament for Pahiatua in 1943 and held the seat until he retired in 1977. During his term of office, times were generally good economically and he was a master of consensus. However, he stopped All Black teams going to South Africa without Maori players, dealt shrewdly with US demands for troops for Vietnam, advanced the agreement towards free trade with Australia, and had to cope with imminent British membership of the European Economic Community.

disadvantages suffered by Maori. He also began the anti-nuclear policy by banning the testing and even the storage of nuclear weapons in New Zealand territory. He formally protested against French nuclear tests in the Pacific.

Personally, Holyoake was an amusing and companionable man, an amateur magician who would sometimes stop by at the press gallery to play cards and do a few tricks. He often walked to work on his own, stopping to exchange racing tips with a Chinese greengrocer. He had a listed telephone number at home for many years, sometimes answering it himself. The two crises that impinged on his tenure of office were the Vietnam War and Britain's move into Europe.

The ANZUS and SEATO treaties, his and his party's antipathy to Communism, and trade considerations convinced the New Zealand government to support the American war in Vietnam. Although troops were already serving in Malaysia and Borneo, the government sent an artillery battery to Vietnam in 1965 and made the war an issue in the 1966 election. Holyoake's public support covered a private concern about the war and he committed as few troops as possible to placate American requests. He avoided the large, conscripted troop echelons sent by Australia. Over the following five years, 3890 New Zealand artillery, infantry, Special Air Services and training units served in Vietnam. Thirty-five died and 187 were wounded.

But at home during the 1970s, protests gradually increased with thousands joining a worldwide cause against the war.

For Holyoake and New Zealand, 1967 was a watershed year. A recession bit into the economy; a referendum opened up the licensing laws by approving ten o'clock closing; the country switched to decimal currency; and a New Zealand–Australia Free Trade (NAFTA) agreement was launched, although it was only a few faltering steps towards a barrier-free Tasman – a gesture towards a future of diversification into manufacturing.

The recession was caused by a commodities price slump opening a deficit between export returns and import payments that yawned into an alarming chasm. The currency was devalued. Although the country had experienced roller-coaster export-import balances many times, this was the most precipitous dive since World War II. Unemployment climbed to – wait for it – nearly one per cent, which declares how good things had been for so long; but it hinted at what could happen if the British market disappeared. The government sought advice from World Bank experts who reported what every educated New Zealander knew – that the production and bulk export of very few agricultural commodities to very few markets made the economy dangerously vulnerable to cyclical price changes. The need to sell a greater range of products to a wider stretch of markets led to the catchcry of the time: 'Diversify!'

Primary products, most notably wool, meat and milk, had been good to New Zealand and, despite the threat to markets, farmers got better and better at their job. Backed by first-rate, practical, government-subsidised research, by mechanisation, and by a top-dressing industry that flourished after World War II, they doubled production in the thirty years to 1966 while the number working on farms about halved. Superphosphate was available in limitless quantities from Nauru under a three-way deal with the British and Australians (but not, at first, with the Nauruans). Small aircraft, flown mostly by air force veterans, not only raised production on the flats but also fertilised the hills, pushing sheep higher and higher. With the trees removed and grass clinging precariously to otherwise naked slopes, eroded hillsides collapsed and floods rushed through the valleys. Only after this sort of farming became unprofitable in the 1980s, with wool prices slumping and exotic forestry expanding, did the hills again sit in reasonable comfort above the plains.

Engineering industries had been steadily in production since the heyday of gold-mining. The local home and farm market had long been supplied with appliances such as kitchen ranges and milking-machines. The manufacture of footwear, clothing, a variety of building materials, horse carriages, railways rolling stock, and light engineering products had been a part of the New Zealand economy since the 1880s. Towards the end of the nineteenth century, heavy import tariffs were placed on some of these products to protect the workers involved.

During the term of the First Labour Government, and particularly during the war when imports were limited, a number of firms began manufacturing electrical appliances and other light engineering products. The left wing of the Labour Party, led by John A. Lee, had fought during the 1930s for a policy of self-sufficiency with exchange controls, protection for developing secondary industries behind import licensing and tariff barriers (which had been used to develop industry in the United States and other nations), backed by the issue of credit by the government. The issue was divisive within the party, rejected as it was by the more cautious Savage-Nash-Fraser triumvirate. But a problem here for manufacturers was the small size of the domestic market which made economies of scale and competition difficult. Also, companies were too small to resource research and development. That it could be done, though, has been proved by some – notably Fisher and Paykel which began manufacturing in 1939 – but it took the opening of the Australian market for them to flourish.

Although the economy remained fundamentally dependant on agricultural products after the war, farming continued to stimulate a number of processing and light engineering industries which helped create jobs as the number of workers needed on farms diminished. On-farm mechanisation and more intensive stocking promoted the development of sophisticated fencing systems, milking machinery and even the manufacture of light aircraft at the height of the top-dressing boom.

Forestry emerged as a significant export industry. It dates back to the 1880s when a school of forestry was established by Premier Julius Vogel. Exports to Australia of native timbers at this time were huge, mainly through the Melbourne-based

Kauri Timber Company. A few *pinus radiata* plantations were planted as early as the 1870s but it was in the 1920s that a great expansion of state exotic forests took place and laid the foundation for the future export of logs and for the manufacture of pulp, paper and light building products. New Zealand has an ideal climate for the early maturing of Californian pines, thus providing sustainable crops. The Tasman Pulp and Paper Company was set up in 1952 to use timber from the Kaingaroa State Forest, once touted as the largest man-made forest in the world. Since then, the industry has become an important part of the economy.

Steel from the black ironsands of the North Island's west coast began production in the late 1960s. An aluminium smelter at Bluff took advantage of cheap and abundant electricity, and a carpet industry based on the strong wool from cross-bred sheep gained export momentum. Free trade arrangements with Australia stimulated short-run manufactures of, for example, electronic products for niche markets.

British Prime Minister Harold Macmillan (1957–63) visited New Zealand in 1958 (seen here greeted by King Koroki at Turangawaewae Pa), a time when Britain was awarding independence to many former colonies and retreating as a world power. He failed at the first attempt to join the European Community. When he made his famous 'wind of change' speech, it presaged great change in New Zealand's future as well.

But a spectre that haunted the future of farming as the 1960s ran their course arose from Britain facing the truth that after the war it had shrunk from a world to a European power. As it pulled back from its old imperial boundaries, Prime Minister Harold Macmillan, in February 1960, resoundingly referred to 'the wind of change' that was blowing over Africa. That wind was blowing New Zealand's way as well, laden with the most serious challenge the country had faced in a century. First, as Britain withdrew forces from the Asia-Pacific region, New Zealand had to look warily towards closer ties with the United States and Australia for regional security. Secondly, and much more ominously, Britain's proposed link to the European

167

Economic Community (EEC) would bring to an abrupt end a trading relationship that had persisted through wars and depressions since refrigerated shipping was introduced in the 1880s – a link on which New Zealand had built prosperity, but also a dangerous dependence.

With Europe forming an economic bloc, Britain would need to drop a drawbridge across the channel that had been the moat around its castle for centuries; or it would be dwarfed by, and shut out from, an enormous neighbouring market. The French twice blocked British attempts to join but, by the middle of the 1960s, New Zealand accepted that eventual membership was certain. Not that Kiwis weren't nervous about it and even a bit wounded that, after being loyal to the British Empire and Commonwealth beyond any other country, they could so lightly be cut adrift. The alternative was to confront our geographical reality and build a trade base around the Pacific rim and Asia, notably with the burgeoning Japanese post-war economy. For many older New Zealanders, rejection by Britain smacked of treachery, and doing business with a country some still saw as the enemy was anathema. But realists got on with the job.

The Deputy Prime Minister 'Gentleman Jack' Marshall conducted negotiations with Britain and the EEC, with Britain's membership imminent. He ably fought a rearguard action to secure an agreement that Britain would continue to take all the meat and dairy produce available for export until the end of 1972. This was a transitional arrangement but he also negotiated access to Britain for diminishing quotas after it joined.

🐝 🐝 🐝

Holyoake's reaction to the need for change was utterly consistent with his political philosophy – don't move until you get people to point the way, and then go slowly. He sought a broad-based consensual indicative plan. Development councils were set up embracing every industrial sector in the country. They plotted a route to the future, and reported in

1969 to a National Development Conference which made more than 600 recommendations through a National Development Council. The work done throughout the country got less credit than it deserved. It pulled together for the first time a lot of information about industrial sectors. It called for diversifying production and markets and enunciated for the first time, officially, the concept of adding value to exports by additional processing within the country. It also marked out the political difficulties involved in further processing products for exporting to countries like Japan and the United States with their intricate sets of trade barriers. It emphasised that because of the traditional bulk despatch of commodities mainly to one market, New Zealanders lacked marketing skills. But the council's recommendations and targets were largely ignored for two main reasons – a sudden, marked recovery of commodity prices, and a change of government when Labour, led by Norman Kirk, won a sweeping victory in the 1972 election with fifty-five seats to National's thirty-two.

John Ross Marshall, known by the soubriquet of 'Gentleman Jack', was Prime Minister for ten months on the retirement from that office of Keith Holyoake in February 1972. Marshall was born in Wellington, graduated with a BA, LLB and LLM from Victoria University and became a barrister and solicitor, and law lecturer. He was an MP from 1946 until 1975 and held many senior ministerial jobs in National administrations. His image was of a man of great courtesy under a veneer of icy calm.

With unpredictable economic currents ahead, the Holyoake government also decided to examine the welfare state. In 1969, a Royal Commission began to assess the state of social security. The report delivered three years later was long and cumbersomely written but its appendices were a rich mine of information. It not only confirmed the worth of the welfare state, it suggested the expansion of the system – from one that provided basic economic and social support to one that would enable beneficiaries to take a full part in the 'mainstream' life of the community. As a result, the government doubled the family benefit, ending the less egalitarian tax exemption for children.

In this last year of its long hold on power, National also brought in extraordinarily inventive accident compensation legislation, providing earnings-related cover for anyone injured at work or on the road. The following year, 1973, the new Labour Government extended the cover to every citizen, including non-earners. Accident compensation was an insurance-style scheme, financed by compulsory premiums from employers, the self-employed and the owners of motor vehicles. It supplanted traditional rights of accident victims to litigate for what may have been negligence involved in the cause of an accident. Over the years, it has strained to keep costs under control and has been amended in many ways – but has survived, perhaps mostly because of soaring civil litigation costs in other, similar, Western countries.

The National Party had been slowly renewing itself with a number of smart young members. Holyoake had talked of retirement and two years after winning the 1969 election he was persuaded to stand down as Prime Minister in favour of Marshall – which was a transition from the old guard to the old guard. A gesture towards redemption was the appointment of Minister of Finance Robert Muldoon as Deputy Prime Minister. You didn't need to be a close observer of politics to know that the clever, ruthlessly ambitious Muldoon would be Brutus to Marshall's Caesar as soon as the chance came. But he would have to wait while 'Big Norm' Norman Kirk took the stage.

The end of the Holyoake years, it's easy to see now, was twilight on a late summer's day, with a blustery autumn and cold winter ahead. Within a few years, the security of full employment, free education and health services had faded away along with relaxed small-town life as young New Zealanders crowded into the cities, particularly Auckland. Crime and anti-social behaviour gradually but insistently grew. Holyoake's own career petered out slowly and then ended in controversy. He stayed in Parliament as Minister of State after stepping down from the top job. Then, in 1977, he resigned after being nominated Governor-General, a political appointment so overt and unprecedented it tarnished his reputation.

When the liquor licensing laws were at last loosened in 1967, a transformation began that has been a revolution. When I worked shifts for the NZ Press Association in central Wellington in the early 1950s, dinner in town was hard to find. Garland's family restaurants served roast lamb and beef with boiled vegetables; some grill rooms – ranging from the ordinary down to the scungy – offered overcooked, shoe-sole steak with eggs, tomatoes and chips. The only fast food available near the office was from Rose's Milk Bar on Lambton Quay – tomato soup from a can, scrambled or poached eggs, baked beans or spaghetti, all with white bread toast. None of the restaurants were licensed and, had they been, only beer or some sort of plonk would have been available. That situation existed around the country and didn't change much until the 1970s when, the dam having broken with the move to ten o'clock closing, the old mores were washed away. The wine and food industry developed spectacularly and within two decades New Zealand moved from a barren brown beer and baked beans world to a nation presenting a varied and good-quality international cuisine, accompanied by wine styles the equal of those produced anywhere. It was an extraordinarily fast revolution, an achievement unparalleled by any other Western country.

Among the stimuli were the jumbo jet that introduced Kiwis to the cuisine and wine of sophisticated cities around the world, and immigration that brought foreigners here. An influx of Dutch, many from Indonesia, had a huge influence in elevating the standard of cuisine in the early years. For generations it had been impossible for restaurants or cabarets to gain liquor licences, so many broke the law. The administration of the laws had always been a bit of a comedy with after-hours drinking and consuming alcohol at dances and balls regarded as a challenge to the Kiwis' vaunted ingenuity. By the late 1960s, though, it had become farce. Some hotels were staying wide open at night, openly signing people in for meals and accommodation to enable publicans to serve drinks to anyone in the bar.

But after 1967, laws that were fossils of nineteenth-century

Norman Eric Kirk led the Labour Party from the wilderness in 1972 when he became Prime Minister in a landslide – but he died in office after only two years. A large, inspirational man, he changed the way the country handled its foreign policy and seemed assured of a long tenure when his health failed following surgery for varicose veins. Kirk was a former engine driver with only a primary school education who became the youngest mayor in the country (of Kaiapoi) at thirty, won the Lyttelton seat four years later and began a rapid ascent to the top of the Labour Party.

puritanism were consigned to the museum of social history.

🌿 🌿 🌿

Norman Kirk had, above all, personal presence. A shade over six feet tall, of ursine build, he could rivet attention with a voice that slipped quickly from soft and insistent to loud and hectoring. His personality was an amalgam of enthusiasm and determination, and when he spoke people watched and listened. He left school at thirteen, but it was clear from soon after his election to Parliament in 1957 at age thirty-five that he was a potential leader.

Backed by trade unions, he made his way through the vice-presidency and presidency of the party. In 1965, he shouldered Arnold Nordmeyer aside and became Leader of the Opposition. Nordmeyer, who started his professional life as a Presbyterian minister, had been a leading Labour MP for exactly thirty years. He was a sharp-witted, keen debater, a decent man cursed by a high-pitched piercing voice and a place in the public memory as architect of the 1958 Black Budget.

Kirk was mayor of Kaiapoi when he first became an MP and his dress and hair-style were very country town. Public relations advisors tried to persuade him to modernise his image but were shrugged away – until Labour lost the 1969 election. Then he took advice, shed four stone, moved into fashionable suits, grew his hair longer and had it styled. This enhanced the warm and earnest manner that gave him impressive television impact. He took longer than his supporters had anticipated to stamp his personality on the electorate. When it happened it caused a landslide.

Although a surge in commodity prices in the early 1970s ended the recession of the previous few years, most of the public could sense an underlying economic malaise and were nervous with a sense of drift under National that had been acceptable during the long years of consistent prosperity. The National Party was tired. Prime Minister for only nine months following Holyoake's retirement, Jack Marshall campaigned shrewdly, emphasising the skill with which he had negotiated on the country's behalf to get continued access to the British market for agricultural products. He was an astute, experienced politician, but inert, cautious, and cold-eyed. In contrast to Kirk, he had the telegenic appeal of a well-turned-out tailor's dummy.

Came 1972, the year before the population reached three million. Kirk was the force that propelled Labour into power with a momentum it had not achieved since 1935. He brought a new idealism to government and especially to foreign affairs, catching a wave of anger against the French for testing nuclear weapons in this part of the world. The government won a case against French Pacific testing in the International Court of Justice – which the French ignored. Next, the administration sent RNZN frigates *Otago* and *Canterbury* into the Mururoa testing zone.

The stand-off with the French came to a head in 1985 when French agents sank the Greenpeace ship, *Rainbow Warrior*, in Auckland's Waitemata Harbour, as it prepared to sail yet again into the Mururoa area. One person was killed,

The Greenpeace ship, Rainbow Warrior, lies against a wharf in Waitemata Harbour, Auckland, after French agents sank it as it prepared to sail to Mururoa, French Polynesia, where the French government was conducting nuclear tests. One Greenpeace worker was killed and two French agents were later captured, tried and jailed.

and two French agents were captured, tried and jailed. This was after later governments had endorsed an anti-nuclear policy invigorated by Kirk that barred even the nuclear-powered ships of allied countries from territorial waters, despite retaliatory diplomatic action by the United States and unofficial criticism from Australia. Australia – abutting as it does the populous and restless nation of Indonesia – suffers an insecurity not shared by its more remote south-eastern neighbour. Since the Vietnam War, New Zealand has given defence less money and attention than previously – to the chagrin of its trans-Tasman neighbour – although it has provided troops for United Nations peacekeeping projects.

Kirk set up warm relationships with African and Asian nations. His government refused visas in 1973 to a visiting Springbok rugby team because the sport wasn't racially integrated. He established diplomatic relations with China. Kirk always seemed in a desperate hurry. His health wasn't good and he worked as though trying to elude a nemesis only he could foresee. After he died following surgery for varicose veins, it became clear he was also suffering from incipient paranoia, a sense that enemies even within his own party were conspiring against him.

In shaping foreign policy, Kirk and his government stepped up to opponents fearlessly and warmly acknowledged new friends in Africa and Asia with an aura of moral rectitude unusual in the world of diplomacy. Most New Zealanders just loved it. When he died only two years after he took office, some of the stuffing went out of the country. In the government's first two years, the economy had buzzed but then, as though grieving at the loss of Big Norm, it sagged and was hit by the first of the oil shocks – surging oil prices that set costs soaring and triggered inflation.

Kirk's Minister of Finance, Bill Rowling, became Prime Minister. He was as small as Kirk had been big, as timid in appearance and speech as Kirk had been bold. It had seemed impossible that a thirty-plus seat majority in Parliament could be squandered in just one term, but it was. Rowling was confronted by one of the cleverest politicians and certainly the most truculent of the post-war era, Robert David Muldoon. Muldoon was a small, pudgy man with a large round head and a scar that twisted his smile up the side of his face, a smile that could appear either sinister or sardonic, depending on his mood. But his ability as a populist to exploit television in pursuit of the 'ordinary bloke' was extraordinary, demonstrating as he did the superiority, even on camera, of a powerful presence over prettiness.

At a personal level, Muldoon sought domination of all potential opponents with a ruthlessness not seen in New Zealand politics for a long time. He belittled the hesitant, inarticulate Rowling by talking down to him, including calling him 'Wallace' (his real first name). His brash, brusque manner offended many people outside politics, especially those liberals who, fresh from the idealism of Kirk, decided Rowling needed help. Some big names among them fronted a 'Citizens for Rowling' campaign, ostensibly to push for the Labour leader, but really to prevent what they saw as the politically vulgar Muldoon from gaining office. With an air of moral superiority and extraordinary naïvety, some mature and experienced people seemed to think that Citizens for Rowling was somehow a civil movement and not a political one. Muldoon soon disabused them.

Labour had inaugurated a compulsory superannuation scheme, the brainchild of Cabinet Minister Roger Douglas. The aim was for New Zealanders to contribute for life to a fund which would build up and from which they would ultimately draw their superannuation. The fund would be under the control of a commission and Douglas saw this as an opportunity to amass a huge pool of money, rich in portent for a capital-strapped country with one of the world's lowest cash-savings rates. Muldoon campaigned insistently that it would be socialism via the back door, that the fund would put unhealthy financial power into the hands of a

Wallace Edward Rowling, known as Bill, took over as Prime Minister on the death of Norman Kirk from September 1974 until Labour's defeat by National the following year. He remained Leader of the Opposition until David Lange replaced him in 1983. A naïve Citizens for Rowling campaign directed against Rob Muldoon during the 1975 election campaign back-fired and probably contributed towards Labour's defeat. Rowling was born in Motueka and gained an MA in economics at Canterbury University. He was an intelligent man, apparently resolute in small groups but came across as hesitant and inarticulate on television.

government. He stormed around the country armed with actuarial charts and graphs and a pointer, dramatically underpinning his argument. At the same time he offered a massive electoral bribe – a scheme in which a pension of up to eighty per cent of the average ordinary wage would be paid from taxation to everyone at age sixty – immediately. That was the hook. The bait was the promise to repay every taxpayer with the money already paid into Labour's fund, reminiscent of Walter Nash's £100 bribe in 1957.

The nation bit. In 1975, Muldoon became Prime Minister. National won fifty-five seats to Labour's thirty-two – a precise reversal of the 1972 result.

Chapter Fifteen:

THE YEARS OF TUMULT

DEEP INTO THE 1970s, New Zealand had a reputation as perhaps the most equable and egalitarian democracy of them all. Then, suddenly, exigent demands for economic and social change pressed upon it as never before. When the crunch came, during the twenty-seven years following the death of Norman Kirk, three leaders attempted to deal with the confusion over the country's changing place in the world – Robert Muldoon, David Lange and Jim Bolger.

Muldoon – an Auckland-born accountant in Parliament for Tamaki since 1960 – and his immediate successor, Lange, were both scintillatingly clever, perhaps the two quickest minds ever to hold the job. Both were compellingly histrionic even among politicians who, in the television age, train as thespians. And yet they were profoundly different in personality and style. Muldoon's political arena was the bullring, Lange's the playpen. Muldoon stung like his contemporary, Muhammad Ali's bee. Lange floated like his butterfly. One was ferociously confrontational, the other evasive, a

Robert David Muldoon was the most controversial Prime Minister (1975–84) of modern times because of his divisive pugnacity and populist policies. His refusal to stop the NZ Rugby Union from inviting the Springboks to tour the country in 1981 provoked anger among a large number of Kiwis and led to fighting in the streets. He was at first dominant over his Cabinet but became increasingly isolated. He was toppled by Labour after calling a snap election. Muldoon was born in Auckland and qualified as a professional accountant, entered Parliament in 1960 as the MP for Tamaki, was Minister of Finance (1967–72), and then Deputy Prime Minister. He deposed Jack Marshall for the leadership in time to become Prime Minister when National won the 1975 election.

counterpuncher. One wielded his wit like a cutlass, the other riposted with a rapier. One dominated his Cabinet for five years as had no other Prime Minister since Richard Seddon, as the pundits liked to write. The other had less and less influence on his colleagues and on his government's policy as the months went by.

In the end, both were failures. One became gin-soaked and was beaten in hand-to-hand combat by a resilient young woman. The other walked away from his ideologue colleagues for a cup of tea.

When Muldoon was under pressure to explain an exodus of 50,000 New Zealanders to Australia during 1977 and 1978, he retorted that those leaving would raise the average national IQ on both sides of the Tasman. With his twisted smile and mirthless laugh, he became a favourite of satirists and a world figure, enjoyed but not necessarily admired. I was once introduced to the poet Paul Muldoon at Princeton University and asked if he had heard of Robert. He replied, grinning: 'Ah, yes, Piggy. He's world-famous among Muldoons.'

Lange, in Parliament for less than three years when elected Deputy Leader of the Opposition under Bill Rowling, became a legendary wit. Almost every time he wrote or spoke, he said something disarmingly funny. A bulky man, he wore his jollity on a good-humoured face but could easily turn an audience his way with his gift for language – as he did during a memorable Oxford Union debate on New Zealand nuclear policy against famous and influential American preacher and politician Jerry Falwell. Lange was a clear winner.

Jim Bolger bore no likeness to his predecessors. He was a plain man, with a Farmer Jim image shaped by his rural background. He was considered, in middle-class Kiwi parlance, dumb. In fact, he was a much more astute and resilient politician than his opponents assumed, often to their cost. He held his government together through three elections before being toppled from within.

The Muldoon years were nothing if not exciting but, sadly, in a way that disrupted discourse and distracted public attention from fundamental social and economic issues. His attitude towards racism seemed sometimes much the same as Queen Victoria's had been towards lesbianism – that he didn't accept its existence even though most people regarded it as one of the scourges of the twentieth century. But to assume that would be to underestimate his sense of where real power lay in New Zealand at that time – among the deeply conservative, rugby-loving people in the provinces and the blue-collar suburbs.

His miscalculation lay in underestimating the growing anathema, even repugnance, in the Western world for racial injustice. And I believe that part of this miscalculation was his failure to understand the growing influence of women. If urban men vacillated on the issue of whether politics should interfere with their beloved rugby, women didn't and their influence was crucial.

The Maori move away from their rural origins had continued. By 1976, more than three-quarters of them lived in towns and cities. Also, the nearly 1000-year-old Polynesian

Police confront angry protestors in Queen Street, Auckland, hours before the NZ Rugby Union made its final decision to proceed with the 1981 tour by the Springboks. Rob Muldoon's National government had refused to intercede, and when the tour eventuated the fighting in the streets between protestors, supporters and police was unprecedented.

migrations had continued until more Cook Islanders, Niueans and Tokelauans lived here than in their native countries. They were able to come and go as New Zealand citizens but Samoans and Tongans were also arriving in unprecedented numbers and were not entitled to automatic access. One official calculation at the time was that 10,000 of them had overstayed their visas, working mainly in menial jobs. As unemployment continued to grow, police and immigration officers moved against overstayers with dawn raids and casual identity checks, actions that smacked of Fascist regimes.

More damaging in the eyes of the international community was the Muldoon government's attitude towards sporting contacts with South Africa. With his colleagues' surprising support, or at least their pusillanimous acquiescence, he refused to intervene when the New Zealand Rugby Football Union decided on an All Black tour to South Africa in 1976. As a result, African and some other nations boycotted the Olympic Games in Montreal. He went further, trying to stare down both internal and international contempt when, in 1981, he refused to stop a Springbok tour of this country and created violence in the streets on a scale unprecedented since the civil war 120 years before. Many foreigners found it hard to understand how a country with so little institutional racism in modern times had come to such a state.

But internally Labour was in disarray and National won the 1978 election with a reduced but still comfortable majority. In 1981, Labour was a shapeless force, ineffectually led by Rowling who was soon to be deposed. National won the election with a majority of one seat. Muldoon had gathered the votes of many previous Labour supporters on the issue of rugby tours but as the 1970s progressed, he became increasingly arrogant and was seen by a growing number of Kiwis to be more trouble than he was worth. In 1980, an attempted leadership coup from within the National Party failed. The government's highly interventionist economic policy had by now disillusioned many of National's traditional professional and business supporters.

In fact, remarkable progress had been made during the previous decade in expanding the range of products and in increasing export markets. Muldoon's government certainly worked hard at a more intimate trading embrace with Australia through Closer Economic Relations, or CER as it was now known, which had supplanted the New Zealand Australia Free Trade Agreement (NAFTA). Exports across the Tasman were increasing dramatically.

Gradually, free trade between the two countries was coming to pass, to be followed by gradual harmonisation of some regulatory legislation to ease inter-country commerce. Indeed, before the century was out, many were talking up the idea of a common currency. Some Kiwis were wondering if the New Zealand economy was big enough to survive in a world in which major trading blocs were gathering. Some even wanted the government to consider concepts of political unity with Australia.

In 1950, nearly seventy per cent of exports went to Britain. This was down to thirty-six per cent in 1970 and below ten per cent by 1985. Exports to Japan had grown from nothing to ten per cent of the total by 1970 and had continued to rise steadily. But perhaps the most striking fact was that by 1980, more than thirty per cent of total exports went to countries other than Australia, Britain, Japan and the US. This trade to an ever-growing number of nations continued. Manufacturing had its place, but the biggest earners were still foodstuffs – dairy products, meat, fruit, fish and vegetables, better marketed than ever before and now processed and packaged with increasing sophistication to appeal to luxury markets.

The country was, nevertheless, deeply in trouble with a convergence of crises: large balance of payments and internal budget deficits, inflation running at more than fifteen per cent and growing unemployment. Muldoon, Minister of Finance as well as Prime Minister, inherited a huge public debt, built up by Labour in its last oil-shock year. It had borrowed overseas to make up for the trade deficit rather than apply the sort of deflationary measures which had traumatised the electorate in 1958. Muldoon simply continued the borrowing he had condemned during the election campaign.

When the second oil shock came in 1979, it brought tough times and the government's answer was increased intervention – more tampering with interest rates, wage levels, dividends and rents, the value of the currency and other manipulable economic factors; although some controls on overseas investment were loosened. The government had developed a policy labelled 'Think Big', based on natural gas reserves, designed to insulate the country from climbing oil prices.

But the most extraordinary move that most dislocated production from markets was labelled Subsidised Minimum Prices, SMPs, by which farmers were paid by the government for stock numbers. The national sheep flock, notionally anyway, soared past seventy million as farmers farmed taxpayers rather than their land. Meat and wool were produced irrespective of demand, pushing land prices up and commodity prices down.

Marilyn Joy Waring was an MP (first for Raglan and then Waipa) from 1975 when she was twenty-three until she retired in 1984. A graduate of Waikato University, she became an outspoken supporter of women's rights, served on the United Nations Commission on the Status of Women, and was leader of the NZ delegation to an OECD conference on the role of women in the economy. She was instrumental in the fall of the Muldoon government in 1984 when she withdrew her support and forced a snap election.

Muldoon temporised in the face of a rapidly changing world, but the almost total dissociation of the economy from domestic and international market forces could not be sustained. A case could be made for subtly managing the economy through gradual change, but the government's almost total control was suffocating. It had hardly deviated from the borrow-and-hope policies of past governments waiting for commodity prices to make their cyclical climb to national prosperity – but the world had changed and the country was far too deeply in debt for that sort of rescue.

National's borrowing for Think Big had further exacerbated the gathering crisis when that mythical year, 1984, arrived. By then, conditions weren't Orwellian, though they were seriously Micawberish – outgoings were far exceeding income. Business interests had abandoned Muldoon and the sycophants in his cabinet, of whom only Derek Quigley had had the courage to publicly criticise policy. The election due at the end of the year would have done for Muldoon and his government, but his nemesis arrived earlier than he had expected.

Government MP Marilyn Waring wanted to speak in Parliament on a disarmament and arms control bill. Muldoon denied her the opportunity so she announced she was withdrawing from caucus and would cast a decisive vote against the government on the issue of allowing nuclear ships to visit New Zealand. On 14 June, Muldoon, stressed and clearly drunk as a television news clip revealed, called a snap election. The New Zealand Party, recently formed by property millionaire Bob Jones, failed to win a seat at the election but won more than twelve per cent of the vote, which certainly helped install a new Lange-led Labour Government with fifty-six seats to National's thirty-seven.

It was appropriate that a woman, Marilyn Waring, mustered up the courage to face down Muldoon and bring the 1984 election forward by four months. Women had made limited and sporadic progress towards equality between the world's first female franchise in 1893 and 1970 when the Women's Liberation Front was formed. The fight for female franchise in the nineteenth century had been led by the intellectually brilliant and redoubtable Kate Sheppard through her membership of the Women's Christian Temperance Union.

Katherine Wilson Sheppard, known as Kate, led the campaign for women's votes as the Superintendent of the Franchise Department of the Women's Christian Temperance Union from 1887. An immensely able and determined woman, she had enormous political influence. She launched five parliamentary petitions seeking votes for women from 1888. The first four were rejected but the last, in 1893, carried the names of one-third of the adult women population, and Parliament duly delivered the female franchise, the first in the world to do so. She was the first president when the National Council of Women was formed in 1896 and became an internationally known feminist as a result of her work here. Born in Liverpool, Sheppard emigrated to New Zealand with her mother and sister in 1869.

183

*Elizabeth Reid
McCombs became NZ's
first woman MP when
she succeeded her
husband, following his
death in 1933, in a by-
election for the Lyttelton
seat. It had been forty
years since women got
the vote. When she died
two years later, her son,
Terence McCombs
became the third member
of the family to hold
Lyttelton for Labour.
Christchurch-born
Elizabeth McCombs was
President of the
provincial section of the
Women's Christian
Temperance Union and
from 1921 until her
death was a
Christchurch City
councillor.*

The WCTU believed women with the vote could bring about national prohibition. A fine speaker and accomplished writer, Sheppard was also inaugural president of the first National Council of Women, and became a world figure as trailblazer for women's rights. But, after Sheppard – and it is a tribute to her remarkable ability – the momentum was lost and women had had to wait twenty-five years from gaining the vote until they won the right to stand for Parliament. Another fourteen years elapsed before Elizabeth McCombs won the Lyttelton seat and became the first woman MP.

The resurgence of the movement came in the 1970s when many groups and alliances came together, educating and informing women from all walks of life. The feminist news-paper *Broadsheet* began publication and became influential. A select committee on women's rights reported on the many areas of inequality. Feminist hero Sonia Davies was elected to the Federation of Labour's executive and then to Parliament. With this kind of backing, women broke clear of traditional condescension from men and marched triumphantly towards equality. They impacted on politics as never before. Sue Wood was elected President of the National Party. Ann Hercus became the first Minister of Women's Affairs. Dame Cath Tizard was appointed Governor-General, Jenny Shipley became the first woman Prime Minister, and Sian Elias the first woman Chief Justice. A large number of talented women caught a wave and rode it into the twenty-first century, dominating politics and the media. In no other country in the world had so many women risen to leadership in almost all spheres of life.

🌿 🌿 🌿

When Labour won the 1984 election it put New Zealand on fast-forward. Lange, who had been in Parliament less than seven years, became Prime Minister. He tended, however, to stand aside from economic issues and left them to his Minister of Finance, Roger Douglas, backed by two associate ministers, Richard Prebble and David Caygill. This trio of radical-right monetarist/supply-side economic theorists needed no urging to effect a policy that became known as Rogernomics. Douglas had given some idea of the policies Labour would adopt in a 1980 book, *There's Got to be a Better Way*, but the truncated election campaign meant most people had no forewarning of the scale or speed of change that started even before the year was out.

The simple unicameral system left after Sid Holland had eliminated the Legislative Council more than thirty years before meant that a majority of Cabinet, unlike almost any other government in the developed world, could push legislation through within hours, if necessary retrospectively.

This was a factor in encouraging the public to endorse a change in the electoral system from first-past-the-post to MMP (mixed member proportional) at a referendum in 1993. Few mainstream politicians wanted to abandon first-past-the-post, especially in the National Party, but the move towards constitutional change had been unleashed by Labour Cabinet Minister and lawyer Geoffrey Palmer. Dissatisfaction at the inability of new small parties to win seats even after attracting a significant portion of the total vote was another factor, and it had not gone unnoticed that Labour had won more votes than National in both 1978 and 1981 but had not gained office.

Douglas was from deep-dyed Labour stock, the son and grandson of MPs, and he would have been familiar with the swiftness of change wrought by new governments at times of economic crisis in the 1890s and, especially, in the 1930s. But what he didn't understand was that in those earlier times the economic malaise impinged directly and painfully on ordinary New Zealanders who wanted something done to alleviate their lot. In 1984, the country was in a bigger mess than it should have been partly because Muldoon's policies had shielded ordinary Kiwis from the direct effects. In fact, inflation had its advocates as they traded up their houses

David Russell Lange, Prime Minister for five years from 1984, entered Parliament for Mangere in 1977, failed in a bid to take over the Labour leadership from Bill Rowling in 1980 and then succeeded in time to win the 1984 election. Lange's confident, quick-witted style buoyed Labour during a period when some businessmen reaped rich harvests from drastic deregulation and many voters suffered losses in an economic crash. But he resigned the leadership in 1989 after sharp differences on policy issues with his Finance Minister Roger Douglas and other senior Labour Cabinet Ministers. He retired from Parliament in 1995. Lange was born in Thames but raised in Otahuhu and qualified as a lawyer in 1965. He is a brilliant, witty speaker and grabbed world headlines after debating his government's anti-nuclear policy with American 'Moral Majority' leader Jerry Falwell at the Oxford Union.

Roger Owen Douglas, the son and grandson of parliamentarians, was the creator of 'Rogernomics' during his role as Minister of Finance in the Labour government that won power in 1984. On taking office, he quickly dismantled a cumbersome regulatory system that had tended to stifle economic enterprise but then shocked the electorate by proceeding to a New Right agenda without built-in protection for investors. He was sacked from Cabinet by David Lange but reinstated by his colleagues, which ultimately resulted in the collapse of the Lange administration. He was later a founder of the Act Party.

and made short-term gains. So, whereas the people received the revolutionary policies of Ballance and Seddon and Savage and Fraser with broad understanding and gratitude, the response to the Lange-Douglas measures was at first bewilderment and then anger.

Perhaps a difference was that in the two previous radical governments, the men responsible had been in politics for a long time, had listened to their constituents over many years, were wary of theory and attuned to practical consequences. Under the Lange regime, what appeared at first to be a shift towards seriously reduced intervention and better management – and Muldoon was right in that governments are always going to be involved in some economic management – became a sharp ideological lurch to the right in which people were left to win or lose according to the caprices of markets.

⚜ ⚜ ⚜

The government immediately devalued the currency by twenty per cent to avoid an exchange crisis, and later floated it. Then, rapidly, the new regime deregulated the financial industry, removed controls on foreign exchange transactions, reformed taxation by dropping the top sixty-six cents in the dollar rate to thirty-three, introduced the Goods and Services Tax (GST) of ten per cent (and soon hiked it to twelve and a half), and removed import licences as well as almost all subsidies, including export incentives and agricultural supports. For farmers it was cold turkey. Those newly on the land with large mortgages were immediately in serious trouble.

The government believed it should get right out of business. Many government trading departments had long been over-staffed, effectively saving workers from what in most other countries would have been unemployment. These trading operations were either turned into stand-alone state commercial operations and told to make profits, or were sold outright, indiscriminately, in many cases to overseas buyers using local merchant banking intermediaries who made extraordinary profits. Included among the sales were Telecom,

Air New Zealand, Petrocorp, NZ Steel, the Post Office Savings Bank (which had been renamed Postbank), the NZ Shipping Corporation and NZ Railways.

Attempts, often unsuccessful, were made to target welfare at only those perceived to need it, to turn state healthcare into a business-based operation, and to decentralise the school system down to local control. Talk of education vouchers to allow parents to buy their children's education wherever they wanted faded away. A surtax on the pension (which continued to be called, inaccurately, superannuation) was an effective means test. Recipients with substantial income from other sources paid their pension back in tax. Local government was reformed with the elimination of a large number of small authorities. The public service was radically changed from its traditional, professional non-partisan role. The government was now able to choose department heads who would be largely in tune with the policies of the government of the day.

For a time there was a public sense of relief that at last a government was acting decisively to fix arcane, outmoded and grossly inefficient administrative structures and to introduce competition among producers and distributors. It also stayed with the nuclear-free policy and with the support of National stoutly opposed a proposed All Black tour to South Africa. Gradually, though, tensions built up between the government – easily the best formally educated and most middle class ever – and the traditional blue-collar Labour supporters. Liberals among the professional classes were also alarmed at the speed made towards hands-off, laissez-faire society. The government eschewed listening to special-interest groups, fearing 'capture', but thus ignored sectoral expertise. Rather, they listened only to what they considered were the pure, clear voices of certain advisers.

Enough support was retained in 1987 when a Labour Government comfortably won a second term for the first

James Brendan Bolger, seen here at a final rally before the 1987 general election which he lost, became Prime Minister in 1990 and was returned in 1993 and 1996 but lost the National Party leadership in Parliament before the 1999 vote. He had a 'Farmer Jim' image but was a shrewd and frequently underestimated politician. Bolger was born in Opunake, farmed in Taranaki and then bought a sheep and beef cattle property near Te Kuiti. He gained the King Country seat in Parliament in 1972, and held a number of Cabinet posts in Muldoon administrations.

time in nearly forty years. But about the time of the election, the stock market crashed in sympathy with others around the world. When the government had deregulated the economy at breakneck speed it had failed to create matching protection for investors against unscrupulous entrepreneurs. Companies that had mushroomed during the government's first term were, in many cases, built on sand. They collapsed and small investors lost their savings.

The government proposed a new economic and social package that included, among other things, a flat rate of income tax and the privatisation of some State Owned Enterprises (SOEs). This came at exactly the time unemployment began to soar and many people considered the main beneficiaries of the Labour economic policy were the wealthy. Overseas buyers were snapping up utilities and the impact was felt for years as profits flowed out of the country, in many cases taken by companies who had no interest in building them up for long-term growth.

The party itself then split into two bitterly opposed factions: those who wanted more concentration on social policy and those who wanted to drive ahead with the New Right proposals. As a one-time staunch Methodist, Lange's political roots were in the Christian socialist movement. As a lawyer in Auckland he had worked with the underresourced rather than rich clients, and he lived an unpretentious life. He realised that he had lost control of financial policy and that the ordinary Labour constituent was being ignored. He sought a pause on the road to the right, suggesting it was time, metaphorically, for a cup of tea.

The second Labour term then descended into internecine fighting of the most undignified kind. Lange sacked Richard Prebble and Douglas. These men with others of the group that engineered Lange's leadership win over Rowling in 1983 then went about engineering his defeat. When caucus re-elected Douglas back into Cabinet, Lange resigned and his deputy Geoffrey Palmer became Prime Minister. A circumspect man, Palmer was unable to weld the factions together into a party with a coherent policy. He resigned less than two months before the 1990 election and Mike Moore took over the leadership.

The National Party won but Jim Bolger was in trouble straight away. He had promised to revoke the surtax on the pension, was persuaded the economy couldn't stand it and welshed on the deal, doing enormous damage to the already tarnished image of politicians. He was also hijacked by the economic fundamentalists in the party, led by Ruth Richardson and Jenny Shipley. Finance Minister Richardson went further down the same path Douglas had trodden in Labour's first term. Facing an enlarging budget deficit, the government attacked the welfare state and imposed a regime of austerity on the country. A pragmatist, Bolger realised he had to get rid of the increasingly unpopular Richardson.

Tensions remained but Bolger held the government together, helped by two unusual men. His deputy was Don McKinnon, a balanced, likeable politician, an excellent facilitator untroubled by ideology or higher political ambition. Number three in the government was Bill Birch, also without leadership aspirations, a functionary who had travelled a curious road, chameleon-like, from being a proclaimed admirer of Muldoon, past the Think Big projects, to economic fundamentalism and believer in the 'trickle-down theory'. These two formed a stable platform beneath Bolger for more than six years.

National seemed almost to have reclaimed its status as the natural governing party having held power for all but twelve of the fifty years since the defeat of Peter Fraser's administration in 1949. But moving up the Cabinet rankings – from number ten in the first Bolger administration to number five in the second – was Jenny Shipley. Backed by younger members, she toppled him before the 1999 election but then fell at that hurdle herself.

Jennifer Mary Shipley became New Zealand's first woman Prime Minister after she ousted Jim Bolger for the leadership of the National government, but then lost the 1999 election to Helen Clark. She was MP for Rakaia from 1987 until her retirement. Born in Gore, Shipley was a teacher before entering politics and successfully held the social welfare, health and transport portfolios during her steady advancement within the parliamentary party.

Helen Elizabeth Clark is New Zealand's first elected woman Prime Minister, winning power as leader of the Parliamentary Labour Party in 1999 and retaining it in 2002. She is tough and smart, and her government has achieved very high levels of public approval with its centre-left policies. Born in Hamilton, Clark graduated with honours from the University of Auckland in 1974, was elected MP for Mt Albert in 1981, held senior portfolios in the 1984–90 Labour administration and was Leader of the Opposition from 1993.

New Zealand moved into the twenty-first century under the command of Labour and Helen Clark. Tough, smart but dangerously susceptible to hubris, she seemed in control, and to her great advantage good times appeared to be here again.

It is a tribute to the stability of the New Zealander's temperament that stable, democratic government emerged intact from the twentieth century after twenty-five years of extraordinary political, social and economic tumult. The population reached four million in 2003, exactly thirty years after it passed three million. It remained a tiny country, bobbing on a huge sea of the world's six billion. The colour of its face was changing, with Maori and Polynesian numbers increasing rapidly in proportion to Pakeha, and dramatically expanding immigration of both ethnic Chinese and Indians, mainly into Auckland.

Although Clark personally and her government achieved very high levels of public acceptance, no one confronting the future had anything like the confidence and optimism New Zealanders carried into the twentieth century, or into the post-war period in 1950. The belief of those times was long gone – that the world was on a steadily rising trajectory of progress and hope towards a better life for all.

In the twenty-first century, what the future held at a time of dizzying change was unpredictable. It left New Zealanders glad of their remoteness but, nevertheless, insecure and uneasy in a dangerously fragmenting world.

TIME-LINE

c. 12 million BC: A strip of land takes its place where New Zealand is.

c. 10,000 BC: New Zealand assumes its present shape and size.

c. 3000 BC: Lapita People move into the fringes of the western Pacific.

c. 1200 BC: Small expeditions of Lapita People have settled in Fiji, Tonga, the Samoas and other islands in the central Pacific.

100 BC **to** AD **200**: The race that evolved as the Polynesians in the central Pacific reach eastwards into the Cook Islands, the Marquesas, the Society Islands and the Tuamotu Archipelago.

AD **200 and 1300**: Polynesian explorers find and settle Hawaii, Rapanui (Easter Island) and New Zealand.

1595: Pukapuka in the Cook Islands discovered by Alvaro de Mendana.

1642: Dutchman Abel Janszoon Tasman sees the west coast of the South Island. His *Heemskerck* and *Zeehaen* anchor in Golden Bay and, after Maori attack a ship's boat and kill four crew the next day, he departs.

1643: Having sailed up the west coast of the North Island and named Cape Maria van Diemen, Tasman's expedition sails back to Batavia without setting foot on New Zealand soil.

1769: Surgeon's boy aboard the *Endeavour* under Captain James Cook sights what is now Young Nicks Head. Cook, Joseph Banks, Daniel Solander and some crew become the first Europeans to set foot on New Zealand, near the site of Gisborne.

Two months later, Frenchman Jeanne-François Marie de Surville arrives.

1770: The *Endeavour* departs for Britain after Cook has completed a circumnavigation of New Zealand.

1772: Frenchman Marion du Fresne and twenty-seven of his men killed by Maori on Moturua Island, as utu for brutality of de Surville.

1773: Cook arrives in Dusky Sound on the *Resolution*, accompanied by the *Adventure* captained by Tobias Furneaux, and returns later to Ship Cove after a journey to Society Islands. *Resolution* is parted from *Adventure*, and leaves for Britain after waiting in vain. Furneaux arrives five days later and some of his crew are killed and eaten by Maori.

1777: Cook arrives aboard the *Resolution* on his third expedition, accompanied by the *Discovery* captained by Charles Clerke. His aim is to discover a north-west passage from the Pacific Ocean to the Atlantic.

1779: Cook killed in Kealakehua Bay in Hawaii.

1792: The *Britannia*, captained by Captain William Raven, lands a sealing party in Dusky Sound.

1805: First cargo of whale oil from New Zealand arrives in Port Jackson, Sydney, aboard the *Scorpion*.

1809: The crew and most of the passengers aboard the *Boyd* in Whangaroa are killed and the ship burnt as an act of utu for the treatment of a Maori crewman of rank. News of this event curbed migrant enthusiasm for New Zealand.

1814: Samuel Marsden lands at Rangihoua, accompanied by missionaries Thomas Kendall, William Hall and others. The day after they land, Marsden conducts the first Christian service in New Zealand.

1820: Kendall, Hongi Hika and Waikato travel to Britain where they meet linguist Samuel Lee and help make Maori a written language, using the English alphabet. Hongi Hika returns to the Bay of Islands with muskets he has bought, and the Musket Wars soon begin in earnest.

1826: Ships of the first New Zealand Company, *Rosanna* and *Lambton*, commanded by Captain James Herd, arrive in New Zealand at Stewart Island with migrants aboard, but the settlement plan is abandoned after the ships visit Otago and Wellington Harbours and the Bay of Islands.

1833: The first British Resident, James Busby, arrives in the Bay of Islands.

1835: William Colenso sets up a printing press at Paihia and produces the first book in Maori, *Epistles to the Philippians and Ephesians*.

Johnny Jones sets out from Sydney to set up a whaling station in Preservation Inlet.

A temperance society is established in the Bay of Islands.

Busby persuades thirty-five chiefs at Waitangi to sign the Declaration of Independence to establish the Confederation of Chiefs and Tribes of New Zealand.

1837: The New Zealand Association, forerunner of the New Zealand Company, is formed in London.

Samuel Marsden leaves for Sydney after his last visit to New Zealand, twenty-three years after he first arrived.

1838: Catholic Bishop Jean Pompallier arrives to establish a mission in the Bay of Islands.

1839: Captain William Hobson, Lieutenant-Governor of New Zealand, is instructed by the British Government to negotiate with Maori for New Zealand sovereignty.

The New Zealand Company advance vessel, *Tory*, arrives and William Wakefield takes possession of land bought in Port Nicholson for the New Zealand Company.

The Nanto-Bordelaise Company is authorised by the French Government to carry eighty colonists to New Zealand.

1840: Governor Gipps formally includes New Zealand within his jurisdiction. Lieutenant-Governor Hobson, after seven days of negotiations with Maori chiefs in the Bay of Islands, signs the Treaty of Waitangi on behalf of the Queen, and fifty Maori leaders sign on behalf of their people. Hobson claims British sovereignty over all of New Zealand, and within a few months the country becomes a Crown Colony under Governor Hobson, separate from NSW, and Auckland is selected as the capital.

Aurora, the first New Zealand Company migrant ship, arrives at Port Nicholson.

Johnny Jones and William Wentworth claim to have bought the South Island and Stewart Island from Maori for £500.

1841: The first settlers arrive in New Plymouth aboard the *William Bryan.*

1842: Governor Hobson dies in Auckland and is succeeded by Willoughby Shortland as Administrator until a replacement governor arrives.

1843: Governor Robert FitzRoy takes up his appointment.

The Northern Wars begin with a series of military engagements at sites such as Ruapekapeka.

1844: Hone Heke cuts down the flagstaff at Kororareka.

1845: Hone Heke sacks Kororareka.

The British government agrees to withdraw FitzRoy after long discontent among southern settlers, especially in Wellington, and is succeeded in November by George Grey, at the end of a term as Governor of South Australia.

1848: The Otago Association founds a Scottish settlement at Dunedin.

A severe earthquake hits Wellington.

1850: The Canterbury Association founds its settlement at Christchurch, and the first four ships arrive.

1852: The New Zealand Constitution Act passed in Britain provides some self-government with wide powers over domestic affairs. Maori policy remains under the control of the Governor and foreign policy under the control of the British Government. Six provincial governments are established (Auckland, New Plymouth, Wellington, Canterbury, Nelson and Otago) with three more formed later as breakaway provinces (Hawke's Bay, Marlborough and Southland).

1853: National and provincial elections held, and Governor Grey leaves at the end of his term. Colonel Robert Wynyard becomes Administrator.

Edward Gibbon Wakefield arrives in New Zealand for the first time.

1854: First General Assembly sits in Auckland.

1855: A massive earthquake hits Cook Strait and raises land on the western side of Wellington Harbour and the Hutt Valley.

1856: Henry Sewell becomes the first Premier, but his administration lasts only a fortnight.

1860: The first battles of the New Zealand Wars are fought in Taranaki.

1861: Gabriel Read discovers gold in Gabriel's Gully, Central Otago, and sparks the first major gold rush.

George Grey starts another term as Governor after governing Cape Colony, and stays until 1868.

A truce is arranged with Maori in Taranaki and Grey begins to move against Waikato Maori.

1864: British troops are involved in the Waikato war against Maori, fighting battles at Rangiriri, Orakau and Gate Pa.

1865: The General Assembly moves to Wellington, which was declared the new capital the previous year.

1867: Four Maori seats in Parliament are created.

Post Office Savings Bank opens first branches in Auckland, Wellington, Christchurch, Dunedin and Hokitika.

1868: William Fox becomes Premier and Julius Vogel, his Colonial Treasurer, soon announces a programme of massive borrowing from overseas to finance immigration and the creation of a railways, telegraph and ports infrastructure.

Te Kooti escapes from Chatham Island on *Rifleman* and sails to Gisborne where he soon begins guerrilla campaign against Colonial forces harassing him.

1869: Government Life Insurance Office set up by Parliament.

1872: Two Maori appointed to the Legislative Council.

1873: Westland becomes a province separate from Canterbury.

1875: Parliament abolishes the provinces from 1876.

1876: A one-man-one-vote Bill introduced by Sir George Grey, now an MP, is defeated.

The provinces are abolished.

1877: Grey becomes Premier, leading his Liberal Party, after a 'Continuous Ministry' led by Fox, Vogel and Harry Atkinson is defeated.

Education Act provides free secondary schooling.

1878: Grey and Sir Robert Stout introduce a Bill to give suffrage for all men over twenty-one. Suffrage for women ratepayers is abandoned after gaining support in both the House and Legislative Council. A campaign to extend the suffrage continues with the support of some conservatives, particularly John Hall.

Railway between Christchurch and Dunedin opened.

1879: Grey's government defeated as a long, intractable depression develops.

1881: An electoral Country Quota is introduced to give rural areas a 33.3 per cent weighting in general elections. The quota was amended over the years and finally abolished by the first Labour Government.

Parihaka attacked and passive resistance leader Te Whiti arrested.

1882: *Dunedin* sails from Port Chalmers for London with the first New Zealand shipment of frozen meat.

1884: The depression continues, and unemployed demonstrate in Auckland. Emigration from New Zealand to Australia and the United States.

1886: Mt Tarawera erupts, kills more than one hundred people and destroys the Pink and White Terraces.

1887: Kate Sheppard of the Women's Christian Temperance Union begins organising a vigorous campaign for women's suffrage.

1889: The principle of one-man-one-vote is established.

1890: The Liberal-Labour Party led by John Ballance wins the general election.

1892: Polynesian Society holds its inaugural meeting.

The New Zealand Rugby Football Union is formed.

1893: Richard John Seddon is Premier following the death of Ballance.

Women gain the vote, the first in the world to do so.

1894: The trail-blazing Industrial Conciliation and Arbitration Act enforces arbitration between employers and employees.

The Bank of New Zealand bailed out from bankruptcy.

1898: The Old Age Pensions Act is passed, the first of its kind in the world.

1899: New Zealand becomes the first colony to sign up for Britain in the war against the Boers in South Africa. The war lasts four years, costs 228 New Zealand lives from 6495 who served.

1900: The Cook Islands are incorporated within New Zealand.

1901: The six Australian colonies federated but New Zealand, invited to join, remains a separate nation.

1902: Seddon's Liberal Party wins a fifth term by 47 seats to 19 and he officially becomes 'Prime Minister' rather than 'Premier'.

1905: Seddon's Liberal Party wins the election by a landslide, with 55 seats to the Opposition's 15.

The first All Black side visits Britain, losing only one game, to Wales.

1906: Seddon dies at sea, returning from a trip to Australia. William Hall-Jones briefly heads the Liberal Ministry until Sir Joseph Ward assumes the leadership.

1907: New Zealand, designated a Dominion, ceases to be a Colony.

1908: The Main Trunk line links Auckland and Wellington.

1909: William Massey announces the Opposition group he leads will be called the Reform Party.

Compulsory military training introduced.

1910: The first New Zealand Labour Party is born at a Trades and Labour Council conference.

Captain Robert Falcon Scott leaves Port Chalmers for his fatal trip to Antarctica.

1911: Population passes one million.

1912: The Liberal Party's twenty-one years in power ends when five members cross the floor of the House to vote with Massey on a no-confidence motion. Four days later Massey is Prime Minister.

Miners' strike at Waihi.

1913: A general strike called by the United Federation of Labour begins in support of a watersiders' stoppage, young farmers on horseback become 'special constables', help work the wharves and are tagged 'Massey's Cossacks'. The 'Red Feds' are defeated, although some strikers hold out until the following January.

1914: World War I breaks out in Europe, and New Zealand Expeditionary Force leaves for Egypt. A contingent of troops sails to Samoa and wrests it from Germany.

Massey's Reform Party wins office by two seats in a general election.

1915: A wartime coalition government of the Reform and Liberal parties is formed.

New Zealand troops take part in the eight-month Gallipoli campaign, in which 2721 of them die and 4752 are wounded.

1916: A new New Zealand Labour Party is formed from left-wing fragments at a conference in Wellington.

1917: New Zealand loses 640 men killed in one day of the Battle of Passchendale, and 2100 are wounded.

Conscription includes Maori for the first time.

Six o'clock closing of hotels is introduced as a wartime measure as political pressure mounts from the Prohibition movement.

1918: Labour Party leader Harry Holland wins the Grey Parliamentary seat and within a few months is joined by Peter Fraser and Robert Semple who win seats in by-elections.

New Zealand troops fight in the Battle of the Somme.

1919: A referendum on Prohibition wins on the day but ultimately fails because the overseas soldiers' votes carry the day.

Massey's Reform Party wins the election that had been postponed for two years because of the war. Michael Joseph

Savage is elected to Parliament for the first time.

1920: The first Anzac Day.

1922: Massey forms a minority government because Liberal and Labour are unwilling to form a coalition.

1925: Gordon Coates becomes Prime Minister as the new leader of the Reform Party following the death of Massey, after an interim administration led by Sir Francis Dillon Bell, and within months Reform easily wins a general election.

First radio broadcast, from Auckland's 1YA.

1926: First family allowances paid by the government.

1928: After a general election, Joseph Ward is Prime Minister at the head of a minority government as leader of the United Party.

1930: George Forbes becomes Prime Minister after Ward's resignation because of ill-health. (He died two months later.)

After several years of recession, the deepest economic depression of the twentieth century descends and lasts five years. 'Relief' of unemployed begins.

1931: Forbes's United Party and Coates's Reform Party forms a coalition which is endorsed at a general election.

The Statute of Westminster gives autonomy to the Dominions of New Zealand, Canada and Australia, and the Union of South Africa, but New Zealand does not adopt it until 1947.

Hawke's Bay earthquake costs 256 lives.

1933: Elizabeth McCombs becomes New Zealand's first woman MP by winning her late husband's Lyttelton seat in a by-election.

Long-time Labour leader Harry Holland dies, succeeded four days later by Michael Joseph Savage.

1935: The Labour Party wins a landslide election victory, Savage becomes Prime Minister and over the following few years inaugurates radical policies including a free health service and a universal superannuation scheme.

Reform and United Parties merge to form the National Party.

1936: National Broadcasting Service established and Parliamentary broadcasts begin.

Guaranteed payments for butter and cheese introduced.

1938: The Labour government is re-elected by an even greater margin after making its radical welfare programme incorporated in the Society Security Act an election issue. Import controls imposed.

1939: New Zealand immediately follows Britain into what becomes World War II, and recruitment begins of a Second New Zealand Division under Major-General Bernard Freyberg.

1940: Fraser becomes the new Labour Prime Minister following the death in office of Savage.

John A. Lee is expelled from the Labour Party.

1941: Second New Zealand Expeditionary Force troops land in Greece.

New Zealand joins the war against Japan.

1942: Conscription of all male British citizens, and women mobilised for essential work.

1943: Labour wins an election postponed because of the war with a reduced number of seats.

1945: War ends first in Europe and then in Pacific.

1946: Labour wins fourth term but this time by only the four Maori seats.

Sir Bernard Freyberg becomes Governor-General.

1947: Labour's Mabel Howard becomes the first woman cabinet minister.

Parliament adopts Statute of Westminster.

1948: Licensing Control Commission set up to regulate liquor licensing.

1949: Referendums favour compulsory military training, but reject extension of liquor trading hours from 6 p.m. to 10 p.m.

Sidney Holland becomes Prime Minister as leader of the National Party which comfortably wins the general election against a Labour Party in decline.

1950: The Legislative Council is abolished.

Petrol and butter rationing cease, and some land sale regulations lifted.

Peter Fraser dies, and is succeeded by 68-year-old Walter Nash two months later as leader of the Labour Party.

Kay-force leaves for the Korean War.

A wool boom begins and causes intense inflationary pressure.

1951: The waterfront dispute, which was to last for 151 days and divide the nation, starts. A state of emergency is declared by the government and servicemen are used to work the wharves.

National calls a snap election and wins easily after a boisterous campaign.

1953: Queen Elizabeth II and Duke of Edinburgh tour New Zealand.

Edmund Hillary and Sherpa Tensing complete first ascent of Mt Everest.

Population passes two million.

Lahar knocks train off bridge at Tangiwai and kills 151.

1954: National retains government.

1957: Sidney Holland retires and Keith Holyoake leads National into a general election. Labour wins with a majority of one seat and Walter Nash becomes Prime Minister.

Sir Leslie Munro of New Zealand is elected president of the United Nations General Assembly.

1958: Labour, with Arnold Nordmeyer as Minister of Finance, introduces its infamous Black Budget, increasing taxes on beer, tobacco and petrol.

Pay-as-You-Earn (PAYE) introduced for income tax.

Edmund Hillary reaches the South Pole, travelling overland.

1959: Auckland Harbour Bridge opens with two lanes.

1960: Keith Holyoake leads the National Party to power and he remains Prime Minister for twelve years.

Peter Snell and Murray Halberg win Olympic gold medals.

1961: Four colleges of the University of New Zealand become separate universities.

Author and publisher A. H. Reed walks from North Cape to the Bluff at the age of eighty-five.

1962: New Zealand and Japan sign a trade pact.

Western Samoa becomes independent.

1964: Marsden Point oil refinery near Whangarei opens.

Peter Snell wins Olympic gold double in 800 and 1500 metres.

1965: New Zealand/Australia Free Trade Agreement (NAFTA), the first steps towards free trade between the two countries, is signed.

Holyoake announces support for the United States in Vietnam, and small combat force despatched.

The Cook Islanders gain self-government but retain New Zealand citizenship.

1967: Decimal currency introduced.

Hotel opening hours extended from 6 p.m. to 10 p.m. after fifty years.

1969: Oil strike off Taranaki coast.

1970: Departure of All Blacks for South African tour draws protests.

1971: Aluminium smelter at Bluff starts operating.

1972: Holyoake retires as Prime Minister, succeeded by his deputy John Marshall.

Norman Kirk becomes Prime Minister when Labour sweeps into power with fifty-five seats to National's thirty-two.

Container shipping services start between New Zealand and United Kingdom.

1973: New Zealand joins OECD.

Colour television introduced.

First steps taken towards equal pay for women.

1974: Prime Minister Norman Kirk dies, is succeeded by Bill Rowling.

1975: Robert Muldoon sweeps to power in the general election, and soon dismantles Labour's funded superannuation scheme for one funded from taxation.

Waitangi Tribunal established.

1976: Pricing subsidies on bread, butter, flour and eggs abolished, and those on Post Office, railways and electricity reduced.

NAFTA extended for ten years.

Butter export quotas to EEC negotiated to 1980.

Protests at visit of US nuclear warship *Truxton*.

African nations pull out of Montreal Olympics in protest at New Zealand's sporting associations with South Africa.

Population officially passes three million.

1977: Holyoake becomes Governor-General.

1979: First stage of production from Maui gas field.

Air New Zealand DC-10 crashes into Mt Erebus in Antarctica with loss of all 257 aboard.

1980: Saturday trading legalised.

Registered unemployed total passes 40,000.

1981: Springbok rugby team tours amid protests and riots throughout the country.

Passports introduced for travel between Australia and New Zealand.

1982: CER (Closer Economic Relations) agreement signed by Australian and New Zealand, and free trade across the Tasman opens up.

1984: Prime Minister Muldoon calls a snap election in July and loses power to Labour led by David Lange, who devalues the

New Zealand dollar by twenty per cent.

Finance Minister Roger Douglas begins deregulatory policy that becomes known as Rogernomics.

Japan is New Zealand's biggest export market for the first time.

Population of Auckland region passes total for South Island.

1985: USS *Buchanan* refused entry to New Zealand ports because of a new anti-nuclear policy which prohibits entry for ships that may be nuclear armed or powered.

Greenpeace vessel *Rainbow Warrior* is sunk in Auckland Harbour by French agents.

Jim McLay replaces Muldoon as Leader of the Opposition.

Lange debates New Zealand nuclear-free policy with American Jerry Falwell at Oxford Union.

1986: Jim Bolger replaces Jim McLay, who announces his retirement from politics.

Sharemarket booms, setting new price levels month by month.

Goods and Services Tax (GST) introduced.

Homosexual Law Reform legislation is passed.

Rebel All Blacks calling themselves the Cavaliers deceive the public and media by travelling to South Africa for tour.

1987: Labour wins general election by an increased majority.

Share prices drop about sixty per cent in four months, and Labour's popularity rapidly declines.

1988: CER advances towards full free trade with a new agreement signed.

Waitangi Tribunal, now looming large in New Zealand life, upholds Maori claims to Northland fisheries. The government returns Bastion Point land in Auckland to Ngati Whatua and pays $3 million resettlement grant.

Labour government begins to unravel over disputes on how far Rogernomics should advance towards laissez faire, and Lange sacks Richard Prebble.

1989: David Lange resigns and is replaced by his deputy Geoffrey Palmer.

1990: Geoffrey Palmer resigns two months before the general election, is succeeded by Mike Moore.

National wins the general election and Jim Bolger becomes Prime Minister. His Minister of Finance, Ruth Richardson, continues the economic liberalism of Roger Douglas until her popularity wanes and she is sacked by Bolger.

1993: Bolger wins the general election.

1995: New Zealand wins yachting's biggest trophy, the America's Cup.

1996: Mixed Member Proportional representation is introduced. Bolger forms a coalition with New Zealand First led by Winston Peters.

1997: Jenny Shipley deposes Bolger and becomes New Zealand's first woman Prime Minister.

1999: Labour's Helen Clark becomes New Zealand's first elected woman Prime Minister in a coalition with the Alliance Party, a union which does not survive the term.

2000: New Zealand retains the America's Cup.

2002: Clark-led Labour becomes minority government in coalition with Jim Anderton's Progressive Coalition, and with support from the Greens and United Future.

2003: Population passes four million.

New Zealand loses the America's Cup.

INDEX

Page numbers in italic indicate illustrations